NIST 800-160

A Roadmap for 21st Century Systems Security Engineering Success

Mark A. Russo, Ph.D., CISSP-ISSAP

NIST 800-160: A Roadmap for 21st Century Systems Security Engineering Success by Mark A. Russo

Copyright © 2021 Cybersentinel, LLC. All rights reserved.

Printed in the United States of America.

January 2019:   First Edition

Revision History for the First Edition

2019:   First Release

Aug 2021:   Update

DEDICATION

This book is dedicated to the cybersecurity men and women of the Department of Defense and US Cybercommand who protect and defend the Information Systems of this great Nation.

NIST 800-160: A Roadmap for 21st Century Systems Security Engineering Success

---

Table of Contents

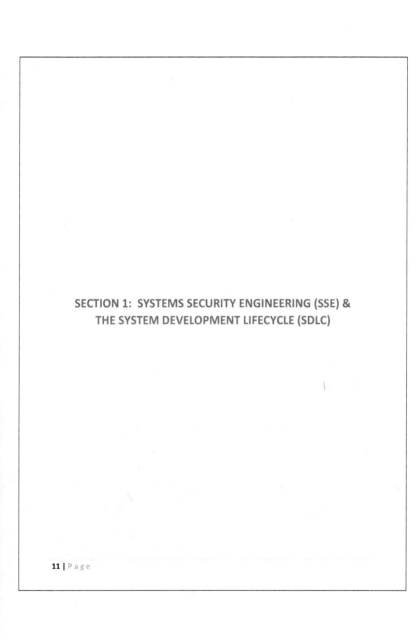

SECTION 1: SYSTEMS SECURITY ENGINEERING (SSE) & THE SYSTEM DEVELOPMENT LIFECYCLE (SDLC)

Systems Security Engineering & NIST 800-160

Function Meets Security

So why is secure system development so hard? It should not be complicated and should follow existing best practices that have been available for decades. It should follow the same path as standard software, hardware, or system development. The disconnect between security requirements, as formulated as a "security control" and the systems engineering process, is at the core of the current break-down. Systems engineering is the foundation of all development efforts. It translates the sought general functionality into a technical specification. For example, a possible function for a modern-day tank is to fire a round for a "threshold" distance of 5 kilometers with an "objective" range of 6 kilometers. The Systems Engineer takes the base functional requirement of "shooting a high explosive round" to a specified and measurable distance. In the case of security, an example of a specified security control would state that all "data at rest be encrypted." The Systems Engineer would take this general requirement and define it better with, for example, "employ a 256-bit AES symmetric encryption application." Unfortunately, this obvious connection typically does not occur—until the very end when the system is already built!

The next chapter will look at a defined process flow that parallels the System Development Life Cycle (SDLC) process. It will take the reader and developer to a clearly defined flow from need to requirement and operational and security functionality traced from beginning to end. The objective is to provide a foundational process that everyone involved in secure system development can follow and appreciate.

While many believe that this process is already understood and wholly adhered to by major businesses and governments, this is far from the truth. The effort here is to educate those overseeing cybersecurity development contracts and to ensure the ability to recognize good engineering processes that meet defined requirements.

What is Systems Security Engineering?

NIST 800-160, *Systems Security Engineering (SSE)*, provides the strategic overview of the SSE process; however, it fails to give practical help and direction to users that desperately need better guidance than best practice suggestions. ***This is not a condemnation*** of NIST's excellent work in this area for years but is an unfortunate rebuke. NIST's works are too academic and strategic to be implemented by novice companies and agencies. This book is written to provide several major and minor tactical frameworks and approaches. It is designed to help businesses and agencies create a secure IT system, network, and environment.

Systems security engineering is a sub-set of Systems Engineering (SE); however, a Systems Engineer's process is no different from SSE. SSE provides the foundation for a structured method to engineering and creating a "trusted" and secure system. "Trust" implies that required or critical security functional requirements needed for a component, subsystem, system, network, application, mission, or enterprise are an integral part of the target entity.

A trusted system is a system that meets specific *security requirements*. *SSE* provides the needed balancing engineering capability that provides security trust to the target system entity. The particular scope of security must be clearly defined by the functional security requirements by the user, system owner, and stakeholders, collectively, regarding the assets to which security applies and the consequences against which security is assessed.

SSE contributes to a broad-based and holistic security perspective and focus. SSE actions use standard and accepted systems engineering and security principles, concepts, and techniques to leverage, adapt, and supplement the relevant principles and practices. These actions are performed systematically to produce acceptable outcomes at every phase of the SDLC.

NIST 800-53 is too cumbersome

In the age of lean and agile development, can SSE and "Agile Cybersecurity" fit into these paradigms? Is it possible to take the complexity of security controls and measures from the varied National Institute of Standards and Technology (NIST) frameworks to keep pace with the demands for agility? We will suggest it is possible to use these already defined "security functionality controls" and directly convert them into typical technical specifications.

Furthermore, if we determine, based upon the current mainstream direction from NIST to establish such standards, a hybrid solution is necessitated. We will provide a "roadmap" to transition to good and secure system development best practices for several candidate frameworks discussed in this book. Agility already exists within the frameworks discussed, and they will be highlighted throughout this book.

Considering the strengths and weaknesses of the "agile" versus the "non-agile" cybersecurity frameworks, agile is a distinct possibility when the processes and principles described in the next chapter are effectively employed. While NIST 800-53, revision 4, *"Security and Privacy Controls for Federal Information Systems and Organizations,"* specifically, is a cumbersome and bottom-driven approach to cybersecurity, it has distinct advantages and disadvantages within secure system development.

We should also consider the advent of the National Cybersecurity Framework (NCF), NIST 800-171, the System Administration, Audit, Network and Security (SANS) Institute (a non-NIST based) solution, and the Health Insurance Portability and Accountability Act (HIPAA) as the most likely to inject agility to the system and software development processes. These are the significant candidates most likely to ensure solid cybersecurity protections and meet the rapidity called for by agile development; the hope lies with these faster-moving solutions than NIST 800-53.

These frameworks and their associated strengths can be contrasted to NIST 800-53. These "agile" approaches have a defined set of top-down and global controls that affords actual simplicity that may be where cybersecurity must go to remain viable. These controls more efficiently address and limit the significant risks and threats affecting the cybersecurity environment across the nation and the globe; while not as all-encompassing as NIST 800-53, the immediate solutions rest with these four major approaches depending in part to their unique IT environments.[1]

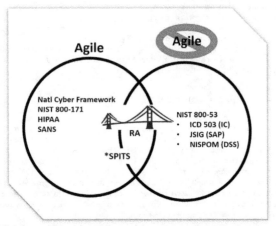

"Agility" Cybersecurity Framework Spectrum (ACFS)

Viewing the advantages of each side of the "Agility" Cybersecurity Framework Spectrum (ACFS) (above), the real agility lies with the simplicity and, more specifically, the *constrained* number of controls on the left side of the ACFS Venn diagram. It provides the broadest solutions for disparate IT systems and environments. NCF, for example, and its brethren frameworks, are ideal to describe an agile environment and address software release/version updates in much shorter timeframes.

Furthermore, the importance and role of the Risk Assessment (RA) will be discussed in a later chapter on how it can be used as an overall "bridge" to inject even greater agility to current cybersecurity processes. For example, compared with NCF, NIST 800-171, and the SANS solutions are far faster to implement than the traditional 800-53 framework. The RA offers even a speedier mechanism, already an inherent control derived from NIST 800-53.

---

[1] For example, HIPAA was created around the protection of Personal Health Information (PHI) and is mandated under federal law as the requited framework specific to the defined "covered entities."

The Risk Management Framework (RMF) Failure

When we discuss any of these approaches, less the SANS solution, they are all governed under the principles of RMF and the NIST 800-series. RMF has been a failure for the federal government's implementation because of the complexity and lack of commitment and resources to implement its guidance truly. The consummate failure of senior leadership and management to adequately resource the cybersecurity effort has been the hallmark of nearly daily reports of another compromise of a network and its precious data. For example, in 2015, the average amount afforded to cybersecurity workforce training at the US Department of Education was $600 per employee per year; the average cybersecurity certification course in the Washington, DC Metro area is over $3000[2]. This reflects the ongoing failure and lack of commitment within the federal government and the downfall from the supposed "home of education" where professional training is afforded short shrift. *How can the private sector solve this problem if even the US federal government treats cybersecurity as a burden?*

For clarification, this failure is no fault of NIST, and the efforts by NIST to create the massive security control listings should not be damned by the negligence of federal leadership in this area for decades. The disappointment lies with senior leadership consistently failing to support its cybersecurity staff and create the needed governance bodies to construct standards.

Leadership continues to express its voluntary ignorance with the "I-am-not-a-cybersecurity-expert" mantra. This has only further eroded the morale within the cybersecurity workforce, anecdotally or not. It represents a concerted lack of interest and desire by leaders at all levels not to recognize that the cyber-threats are real, and leadership's choice to demure its clear ***accountability*** has contributed to the ongoing successes of internal and external threats IT environments. This is consistently reflected in the news with an ever-newer data breach. It has been this complacency that has contributed to the actual state of current cybersecurity: ***failure***.

 The Importance of Threat Intelligence

Constant intrusions into the critical US state and federal Information Technology (IT) systems highlight the ever impactful effects of cyber-threats worldwide (Allyn, 2019; Olson, 2012; Starr, 2015; Stoll, 2005). The 2015 Office of Personnel Management (OPM) cybersecurity attack was one of the most harmful exfiltrations of U.S. government personnel information (Koerner, 2016; Naylor, 2016). Cyber-attacks have also adversely affected the supposedly highly protected networks of the Department of Defense (DOD). "For nearly a week, some 4,000-key military and civilian personnel working for the Joint

---

[2] Based on author's own experience as the Chief Information Security Officer (CISO) at the Department of Education.

Chiefs of Staff lost access to their unclassified email after what is now believed to be an intrusion into the critical Pentagon server that handles that email network" (Starr, 2015, para. 3). The ability to better detect and thwart these cyber-attacks by nefarious threats has not improved even with advances in technologies designed to mitigate these attacks (Allyn, 2019; Garamone, 2018; Mandiant, 2020; Newman, 2020; Stoll, 2005).

Cyber-thugs also hack businesses worldwide (Kaplan, 2016; Olson, 2012). Computer incidents happen to even the most technically knowledgeable firms such as Eurofins, a United Kingdom's (U.K.) based company, in 2019 (Devlin, 2019; Olson, 2012). Eurofins paid an unspecified amount of money to the hackers to regain access to their databases and repositories. This data was paramount to the U.K.'s primary criminal forensics agency in its role to provide advanced technologies to its vast array of Britain's law enforcement organizations (Devlin, 2019). Worldwide technically-focused agencies also continue to fail against ongoing cyber-attacks. International companies' ability to detect and stop an active threat's effects remains incomplete in the ongoing battles in cyberspace (Allyn, 2019; Garamone, 2018; Olson, 2012; Stoll, 2005).

Ezeife, Dong, and Aggarwal (2008) describe the frustration and the level of effort needed to defend against relentless cyber-intrusions. The requirements to monitor threats and update threat data sources, lists, and reports are labor-intensive activities (Darktrace, 2019c; Ezeife, Dong, & Aggarwal, 2008; Homeland Security Systems Engineering and Development Institute [HSSEDI], n.d.; Hurley, 2018). Manual efforts focus on detecting-- and not always preventing-- a cyber-threat incursion into an organization's IT environment, i.e., network. Ezeife et al. (2008) further describe the need to maintain information that includes signature databases used to identify threats as requiring "a lot of human involvement" (p. 98). The need for more capable advanced solutions and an understanding of the strengths of emergent technologies are critical to any future success within active cybersecurity defensive measures (Ibor, Oladeji, & Okunoye, 2018).

Furthermore, the U.S.'s Defense Industrial Base (DIB) provides contract goods and services to the DOD. The DIB faces the same issue of frequent cyber-assaults against its corporate IT infrastructures (Garamone, 2018; Hensel, 2016). These companies must balance national security protection requirements with their financial stability and the knowledge that they are valuable targets to the enemy (Hensel, 2016). Businesses also face growing federal regulatory demands to protect critical DOD-provided information and comply with ever-growing federal cybersecurity rules and regulations (National Institute of Standards and Technology [NIST], 2014; 2015; 2018).

Federally-driven requirements are cumbersome and add to the stress of protecting vital IT assets and capabilities (Ezeife et al., 2008; NIST 2014; 2018). They impact international supply chain participants that must conform to these explicit best practices and contractual requirements. Organizations must continuously secure and remain aware of their sensitive networks and data from cyber-threat nation-state actors engaged in global cyber espionage.

Persistent dangers include what is termed by the DOD as Advanced Persistent Threats (APT). They include China, Russia, Iran, and North Korea and are recognized as significant risks focused against the U.S. and its interests (Clarke & Knacke, 2014; Mandiant, 2013; Olson, 2012; Starr, 2015). These enemies frequently seek insight into DOD and U.S. federal intentions, activities, and efforts against their respective countries

(Garamone, 2018; Hensel, 2016; Starks, 2019). Preventing successful cyber-attacks by these nation-states poses a substantial concern to the DOD and the global community (Clarke & Knacke, 2014; Mandiant, 2020; Olson, 2012; Starr, 2015).

Specifically, industries and governments have poorly leverage threat intelligence to prevent cyber-threats and their negative impacts on their sensitive networks and data (Bala, & Nagpal, 2019; Manjunatha, Gogoi, & Akkalappa, 2019; Starks, 2019; Zuech, Khoshgoftaar, & Wald, 2015). Any solution to the cybersecurity challenge must be contemporary and nimbler against cyber-assaults from the global threat community (Ibor et al., 2018; Mandiant, 2020).

Risk versus Threat

What are the differences between risk and threat? A **threat** is a subcomponent of **risk** and is overall related to the first step of risk management and assessment. Once identified, two significant actions should occur by the System Owner (SO), i.e., the company or agency. The first, and more preferred, is to address and fix the vulnerability as soon as identified. If not possible, the cybersecurity professional will need to develop the core risk management vehicle, the Plan of Action and Milestones (POAM). Recognizing either of these components and documenting their existence MUST be captured and managed with a POAM.

The POAM provides a disciplined and structured method to reduce, manage, mitigate, and ultimately address an active finding/vulnerability. This remaining risk is known as residual risk. This risk exists until the vulnerability is wholly addressed. It may also be accepted and managed during the system's life by the SO and their support cybersecurity professionals.

Specifically, POAM's provide findings, recommendations, and actions that will correct the deficiency or vulnerability; it is not just identifying the risk but having a "plan" that reduces the dangers to a *subjective* determination by the system owner that the control *is met*.

Risk	Threat
Definition	**Definition**
A measure of the extent to which a potential circumstance or event threatens an entity, and typically a function of (i) the adverse impacts that would arise if the circumstance or event occurs; and (ii) the likelihood of occurrence. Information system-related security risks are those risks	Any circumstance or event with the potential to adversely impact organizational operations (including mission, functions, image, or reputation), organizational assets, individuals, other organizations, or the Nation through an information system via unauthorized access, destruction, disclosure,

that arise from the loss of confidentiality, integrity, or availability of information or information systems and reflect the potential adverse impacts to organizational operations (including mission, functions, image, or reputation), organizational assets, individuals, other organizations, and the Nation.	modification of information, and/or denial of service.

A POAM identifies the overall managed *risk*. Many confuse risk with **threat** and use the terms interchangeably. A threat can be an *intentional* threat such as a hacker or an "insider threat" such as a disgruntled employee. *Unintentional* threats can be an accidental transmission of sensitive data or even a natural disaster such as hurricanes or tornadoes. The standard cybersecurity equation for **risk** can be computed as follows:

$$RISK = Threat \ X \ Vulnerability \ X \ Consequence$$

Finally, the POAM is a crucial tool to manage the risk over the life of the system's operational existence. The RMF created by NIST is based on active knowledge, recognition, and a plan to be addressed by the business or agency to provide a reportable and repeatable mechanism that creates the real success of the concept of "risk management." This is not "risk elimination;" it's about an active means to manage risk and any associated threats over time.

The POAM identifies:

- The tasks (initial milestones) need to be accomplished with a recommendation for completion after the Information System's (IS) implementation.

- The scheduled completion dates the company has set for the POAM actions to be completed; should be typically no more than one year, with the possibility of extension as agreed to between the business and the Contract Office.

A Return to the Past: A Hybrid Solution

To fix many of these shortfalls, a return to a balance between risk and threat-based approaches is needed to manage an ever-evolving threat environment. There also needs to be traceability (see the Chart "Risk-Threat Response Workflow"), between "threats" to "risk" to "security controls." The risks are predominantly only tied to security control shortfalls and have further strayed from integrating viable threats in cyberspace as another element lost with the *risk-emphasized* focus of the predominant RMF approach; risk and threat need to be understood and captured by the RMF process in a Risk Assessment Report (RAR) that is updated at least annually. One failure has been that many treat RMF as a once-and-done approach that has only increased the vulnerability of static protections and control mechanisms. Leadership should review at least annually but certainly more often is preferred to diminish the rate of success from varied and ever-evolving threats.

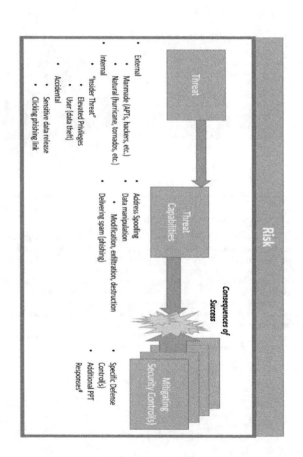

Risk-Threat Response Workflow

A return to threat-based considerations and how they impact risk is essential to move to a more proactive condition. This is a strongly suggested hybrid move from a total focus on just managed risk. A threat can be natural or artificial. It is the manmade variety that is a common concern to the cybersecurity defense community. As the threats are identified, they need to be cataloged typically in a RAR. A RAR is required during the early stages of system development but has not been an everyday activity by program managers or developers alike.

To be more responsive to these threats, consideration must be made regarding hacker capabilities such as stealing log-in credentials, exfiltrating user data, or just plain destruction; it is necessary to identify threat capabilities to the best of the abilities of the system developer and the system owner. It must be "baked-in" *up front*, but woefully most federal IT systems are developed and deployed with no consideration of cybersecurity protections until the very end of the system development lifecycle; that is far too late and is a prime source of disconnect within the public and private sector's efforts to defend their precious data.

Threat capabilities should then be matched against available controls such as those enumerated by NIST. In the case of the NCF, there are 108 controls. The system developer should review whether one or several are needed to reduce or eliminate the threat based upon the initial RAR and any updates performed by the supporting cybersecurity staff to include assigned Information Systems Security Officers (ISSO) and Managers (ISSM).

While it is not always possible to eliminate a threat, every effort should **overwhelm** the threat capabilities with additional controls. In some cases, it may be necessary to turn to NIST 800-53 and its more significant number of candidate controls where the shifting risk-threat environment has changed.

Furthermore, the more constrained and agile frameworks have "globally" identified and generalized risks to a simpler state. While it does not have the more expansive concern of connecting risk and threat accordingly, it is this first step that we suggest needed before we move to a more security-heavy solution such as NIST 800-53—*"we need to walk before we run."* We need to bring the leadership and cybersecurity workforce to a basic standard of 100-200 well-implemented controls before attempting to implement 400 to 800+ poorly executed controls. The effort must educate the public and private workforces more effectively than accepting risk without any appreciation for truly protecting the respective IT environment.

The Nature of Continuous Monitoring

The concept of "continuous monitoring must further match this effort." (See Appendix B). Unfortunately, the approach has been a historically "once-and-shelf" approach that again has only contributed to weak past, present, and presumably, future states of cybersecurity.

Risk Assessments (RA) need to be continuously accomplished and be used to update the RAR as an artifact of record and reference for System Owners (SO) and their IT support staff. Continuous Monitoring ensures a secure state of a company or agency's networks and data by providing an active review vice a "once-and-shelf" approach that has contributed to the current unfortunate state of cybersecurity.

Finally, the guiding principle should consider the "Consequences of Success." *What if the hacker (threat) can complete the exploit?* What are the impacts of qualitative (e.g., loss of customers) and quantitative (e.g., funds siphoned to foreign accounts)? In considering controls matching a threat, the organization must consider, document, and act upon the recommendations that can best reduce the risk to the IT system. The RAR must be a continually maintained document that can be used to identify threats, prioritize future efforts, and identify the timing of funding to meet ongoing and evolving dangers to the IT environment.

SECTION 2: HOW TO FIX SYSTEMS SECURITY DEVELOPMENT?

Cybersecurity Implementation and the SDLC

The A/SDLC and SSE

As discussed in the previous chapter, secure and agile system development are possible; however, "bad practices" still exist in both the public and private sectors and provide an illusion of proper security. The daily intrusions into various corporate and governmental systems and data stores demonstrate that the battle is lost. Much of it is due to the lack of commitment by senior leadership to properly resource its internal cybersecurity organizations and the voluntary disconnect of those charged with program and system development. These individuals and sections chose to avoid and defer to their cybersecurity staff vice supporting them with an active desire to learn and appreciate what secure system development requires.

We introduce a workflow that is not just about security but also about creating a holistic solution for secure system development. It must be ingrained into the process vice being an afterthought where the system is deployed with hundreds of discrete vulnerabilities and shortfalls. The only way that secure system development will improve is when real and understandable system development models incorporate security *and* standard functionality requirements into a singular process—that's where we will start.

In the upper left corner of the diagram below, it starts with validated needs that create specified requirements. They are typically general; for example, "the car must drive non-stop for 650 miles on a tank of gas." How Systems and Hardware Engineers translate, that may include a technical specification, sometimes called a standard, of using a "six-cylinder diesel XYZ engine with electric assist." For security, a common control requires "two-factor authentications." This could include a hard token (i.e., card inserted into a reader) or a text from a merchant's automated system that sends a rotating Personal Identification Number (PIN) to a customer to ensure the security of the transaction.

Suppose you do not have well-defined requirements early. In that case, it will be reflected, at a minimum, as an incomplete solution to the problem the technology created was initially supposed to solve.

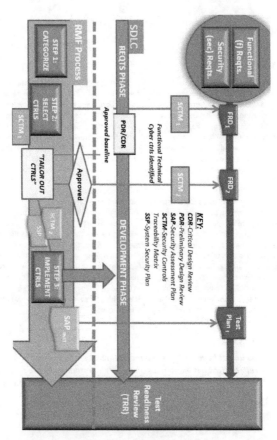

The Integrated Operational-Security SDLC Process

As we proceed to the right, operational and security requirements are combined into a Functional Requirements Document (FRD). A designated program or project manager typically creates the functional requirements, and the security requirements flow from the selected or mandated security framework. This book discusses those frameworks predominantly used within the federal government and many parts of the private sector; we have already discussed these frameworks in general from the previous chapter. Specifically, we will discuss them as the best choices to inject security and agility solutions to affect secure system development.

- **The National Cybersecurity Framework (NCF)**

- **NIST SP 800-171, *Protecting Unclassified Information in Nonfederal Information Systems and Organizations***

The functional requirements are extracted from these NIST publications and should be an integrated component of an overall FRD.

GOING DEEPER

This is an example of security control from NIST 800-171 that requires a technical solution.

"3.11.2 Scan for vulnerabilities in the information system and applications periodically and when new vulnerabilities affecting the system are identified."

It tells you "What" needs to be done but does not describe a solution ("the how"). Here, engineers need to identify technical solutions, such as a "vulnerability scanner" from many available vendors in this arena. This functional description should then be translated into a candidate technology such as: "We will install in the Hot-Mess System the ABC anti-virus/anti-malware solution to address security control 3.11.2" that can readily be deployed as part of the overall system development effort.

As refinement and quality control continue early in the lifecycle, the controls are better understood by the program manager, developer, and users, who are integral stakeholders of any system design process. Some are better-refined functions, and others may be deleted based on a specific solution's technical maturity or readiness. In the case of security, there are situations in the control that may be reasonably tailored out.

Tailoring-out of controls result because there is no reasonable way to address the control within the objective design. An example is an initial security control selected by the specific NIST framework requiring that all WiFi transmissions be encrypted. Tailoring-out may be used if there is no Wi-Fi used in the design of the system. This would include the absence of WiFi base stations, antennas, etc. The lack of such a capability not needed by the stakeholders can be removed under the principles of NIST's RMF. Tailoring-out supports the refined and final security functional controls that will not be included in the final[3] FRD.

During this phase of requirements development, there is usually a Preliminary Design/Critical Design Review (PDR/CDR) meeting. The PDR/CDR may be one or several meetings where key stakeholders validate the functional requirements. Depending on the iterative nature of the chosen development process, such as waterfall, incremental, or current agile, the outcome of such a meeting is to approve the system's baseline. This should include all high-level drawings, schematics, and connections throughout the system. Further, this can still be adjusted during the development process, but only through formal program and configuration management processes that authorize the changes.

The Development Phase allows systems, software, and hardware engineers to translate all functionalities into technical specifications. They will rely on established industry best practices to include specified standards. For example, the DOD for several decades established a myriad of military standards (MIL-STD) for many of its weapon systems. These were standard pre-defined and required components, computers, and materials mandated by the DOD or one of the other four Services. Fortunately, over the years, DOD has relaxed those standards more in line with allowing industry to find, create, and implement better solutions if they could equally or better meet the desired requirement.

The parallel RMF effort creates what is called a Security Control Traceability Matrix (SCTM). It is like the programmatic Requirements Traceability Matrix (RTM) that standard PMs understand and employ; it traces the general requirement, "the car must be able to operate under night-time conditions," and that, for example, leads to adding front lights to the automobile. The SCTM becomes the basis of a test plan. The SCTM is expanded to a Security Assessment Plan (SAP); the SAP becomes the foundational document for cybersecurity assessors to report the developer's status of meeting selected security controls. As in the standard SDLC, the SAP would lead to a singular[4] Test Readiness Review (TRR).

The Test Readiness Review

The TRR is a formal entry point before any testing. It could be used for development testing that is usually for a component, application, etc., where the developer has declared that the system, component, application, etc., is prepared for a third-party and independent test that will demonstrate to stakeholders that the requirements have been met and are near-ready to go "live" or operational. A TRR can also be used for a more significant demonstration of its

---

[3] In Agile Development, there is no true final FRD, but it is only a current "sprint" with a defined set of requirements.
[4] While a singular TRR is the objective of the A/SDLC, it still occurs as two very separate events that have only resulted in poor overall secure system development to-date.

overall completeness where it is tested under real-world conditions; this is typically called an Operational Test (OT).

Furthermore, the TRR is the basis for the stakeholders to accept the developer's readiness to proceed to independent testing. Independent testing and evaluation are the same activity that occurs during cybersecurity audits; third-party auditors or assessors determine the completeness of the developer's efforts to meet the stated requirements. There should be no interpretation functional, and security assessors are any different. They perform a validation of completeness against their respective test plans. In the cybersecurity assessors, the SAP is the formal "roadmap" for the assessment.

Below we have provided a sample TRR checklist. Item # 5 highlights an often-missed event on the part of the developers. The test assessors usually develop the checklist to identify critical pre-events and documents prepared and approved by stakeholders. They typically fail to conduct their internal self-assessment of security controls and enter the TRR unprepared to respond to this criterion.

While a self-assessment[5] cannot be used as part of the final determination, most developers fail to conduct this level of testing. If done correctly, it will provide insight into, for example, security controls that are not fully met or implemented. Where those controls cannot be fully fulfilled, a POAM should be identified and created before the TRR. Unfortunately, that is an ongoing challenge for many of the supposed large defense contractors who don't understand NIST's direction and guidance in this area. This is the Number 1 reason most developers fail when assessed by cybersecurity assessors.

---

[5] Under very limited situations a self-assessment under RMF can be accepted, but the author strongly disagrees with this approach until such time the overall development community demonstrates true competence to implement the entirety of their respective NIST framework.

TRR Entry Criteria			
#	Criteria	Met?	Comments
1	Has system been approved by the System Owner (senior business management)? Artifact provided? (Recommended, but not required)		
2	Has hardware, software, and network physical topology lists and diagrams been completed?		
3	Has business assigned an Information System Security Officer/Engineer as a direct interface to the audit team? Name and contact info?		
4	Has Audit team provided preliminary Rules of Engagement (ROE) for the audit?		
5	Have the controls and configuration of the system been verified by a "dry run" ("Self Assessment") ? Artifacts provided (SSP, POA, and any related support policy documents)?		

Also, Rules of Engagement (ROE) should be developed and provided by cybersecurity assessors as part of the TRR. The ROE sets standards and expectations early. We have provided some essential ROE points to include:

- The lead auditor will establish evaluation criteria for the assessment of security controls.

- There is no "partial" control credit; it's either "compliant," "non-compliant," or "NA."

- All controls are subject to inspection; auditors will not be restricted from accessing portions of the facility or system sub-components directly related to the audit

- The auditor may go beyond documentation review and require demonstration when the control is not clearly answered.

- The company/business is responsible for addressing controls.

- The company/business must demonstrate the controls' implementation to include inherited (in the case where the government provides a means to address the control)

- Controls that are not assessed due to company/business not addressing will be marked as non-compliant.

- Controls assessed as non-compliant and not scored before the auditor's departure will be categorized as non-compliant.

- Inspected POAMs must include an expected completion date and mitigations (until a permanent solution is employed).

- All document references will include the document name, version number and date, page number, and section number that addresses the control.

- If a document reference does not address the control, the auditor will categorize that control as non-compliant.

Developmental and Operational Testing

After the stakeholders have authorized testing, it will classically begin with Developmental Testing (DT). All sub-systems, components, applications, etc., should follow this process. For the cybersecurity assessment portion, an audit occurs against functional requirements captured in the SAP. Depending on the completeness, level of risk, and operational necessity, the system will be provided an Authority to Operate (ATO). An ATO allows the system to connect to operational systems, networks, databases beyond its periphery. The ATO forms the foundation of Risk Management—the Authorizing Official (AO) has accepted the level of risk, threats, and issues that may result in a system compromise. The risk rests with the AO, not the cybersecurity assessors.

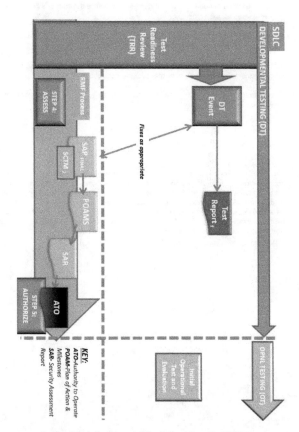

Continuation of - the Integrated Operational-Security SDLC Process

At this phase, the system owner, developer, and operational testing begins. The role of cybersecurity assessors is complete. A final Security Assessment Report (SAR) is issued to the AO with three possible recommendations:

1. Issue an Authority to Operate (ATO)—objective
2. Issue an ATO with Conditions—not optimal and very typical
3. Denial of ATO (DATO) is embarrassing and not usually selected because of the reputational impact on the AO and the developer!

Some forms of cybersecurity Operational Testing (OT) may continue to occur. Most typically, penetration testing identifies systemic problems that variances may miss in testing approaches and methodologies. However, the predominance of this work is completed. The stakeholders will continue to test the system under operational conditions to ensure all system functionality is met and is ready for active use.

The A/SDLC May Be Our Best Hope for SSE

The A/SDLC is the first-ever attempt to integrate the classic life cycle development model with standard NIST frameworks, including NIST 800-53, 800-171, and the newly introduced NCF. It should establish the foundation of improved systems engineering and requirements development processes that ensure security is integral to any current IT-based system design. The objective is to enhance the overall process and bring the leadership and program managers "to the table" to understand cybersecurity's focal points.

It provides a model that is easily understood and provides the graphic representation to help in SSE development. The A/SDLC is a not-so-revolutionary idea created from across the two disciplines of program management and cybersecurity. The A/SDLC may be the best hope to get secure system development as a focus for all of us wishing to operate securely and safely in the Digital Age.

The remaining chapters describe the frameworks of the NCF and NIST 800-171 in greater detail. We also describe the less than understood control of NIST 800-53, the Risk Assessment, and how it can be used during the operations and maintenance phase to manage changes more nimbly. And finally, we introduce the concept of Specialized IT Systems (SPITS), which are IT systems that typically have a particular function. The SPITS require far fewer modifications to cybersecurity accreditation because most security protections are inherited from the central IT system being developed.

The goal is to identify several strategic and tactical frameworks to help the system owner and developer complete an optimally functioning system with the requisite security measures. We discuss their strengths and weaknesses but suggest they all are ideal components of creating an agile and secure development life cycle process.

SSE is already possible. We just need to treat the typical functional and security requirements and their associated NIST security controls EXACTLY the same. We need to stop building security after the fact and make it a defined and integral part of the Requirements and Systems Engineering processes established for decades.

**Stop treating cybersecurity like an after-thought.
Start treating it as a necessity!**

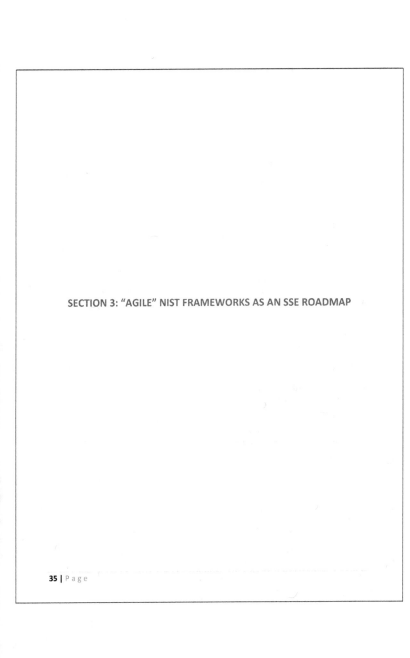

SECTION 3: "AGILE" NIST FRAMEWORKS AS AN SSE ROADMAP

The National Cybersecurity Framework (NCF)

NCF Agility

The NCF is composed of 108 security controls. It is not just the technical aspects but also the managerial and administrative controls that provide a more holistic defense in any NIST-based approach. The **NCF** is currently a voluntary and self-assessed process to inject greater cybersecurity protections into the national security of the US's vital IT infrastructures. It relies upon a concerted effort by the system owner through his developers and security engineers to best determine how to implement the 108 security controls.

The NCF is designed to align its cybersecurity activities with business and mission requirements, risk tolerances, and available resources. While this chapter was developed better to describe the "how" of the control implementation, the NCF can also be used by cybersecurity professionals in both the public and private sector to protect better their most sensitive data and Intellectual Properties (IP). Regardless of their size, risk, or sophistication, it enables organizations to leverage the NCF's principles and best practices as part of an active risk management effort. It provides a common structure and method for effective cybersecurity. It assembles standards, guidelines, and best practices in creating the controls and further aligns them with the critical needs of companies and businesses seeking to secure their IT environments better.

It also reflects an agile model to assist system developers in embedding security within any good cybersecurity program's people, process, and technology aspects. Regarding its relationship to "agile cybersecurity," the NCF affords a relatively good inception of critical controls best suited for supporting transitioning to agile development methods and ensuring agility in the system development process. The NCF control sets developed by NIST are now easily applicable and manageable for both public and private sector cybersecurity protections. It has long been sought by the program management and system development community a better means to secure systems, and NCF will most likely be the most widely adopted beyond the confines of the federal government. The desire is that it becomes the flashpoint to secure the nation's cybersecurity infrastructure better.

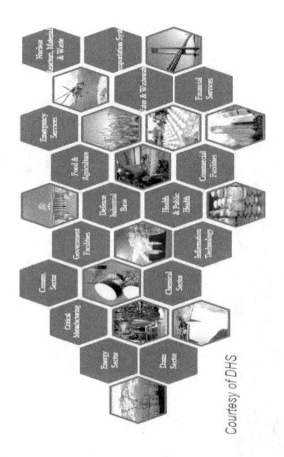

Courtesy of DHS

US Critical Infrastructure Sectors

The NCF is not a "one-size-fits-all" approach to managing cybersecurity risk for critical infrastructure. It affords a level of "agility" to support ongoing cybersecurity threats in the private sector. Organizations will need to continue recognizing the unique risks, threats, vulnerabilities, and risk tolerances that influence their respective sectors; however, NCF is a "lighter" security approach that makes cybersecurity more manageable. The NCF affords the needed control mechanisms to manage and respond to an ever-changing IT threat environment. The guidance provided in this chapter is designed to afford greater nimbleness and afford protections to sensitive systems and data.

	Agile (NCF, etc.)		Not Agile (800-53)	
Its Animal Phrase	"fox-watching-the-hen-house"	Results in poor implementation standards	"A bear to manage."	Cumbersome with as many as 500 security controls
Implementation Direction	*Top-Down	Leverages a global view of threats to IT systems	Bottom-Up	Data drives categorization but allows for "tailoring out "if the control does not make senses (also abused)
Risk v. Threat	*Threat Based	Controls selected based upon global threat to the global IT environment	*Risk-Based	Risk is tied to the level of data sensitivity and controls aligned with greater or lesser protections
Speed to market	*Relatively fast	It can take 1-2 months, and controls can be heavily "POAM'd"	Slow/lengthy	4-6-month end-to-end process
Assessment Process	Allows for Self-	Abuse dangers are the rampant	*Requires Third-	Challenged by IT developers who fail or refuse to follow a framework

	Assessment	*and leading cause of weak cybersecurity practices & protections*	**Party Auditors**

Agile versus non-Agile Advantages and Disadvantages

The asterisked (*) characteristics above are the suggested elements to create a more robust cybersecurity posture, specifically for NCF, and such models as recent implementations of NIST 800-171 by DOD, and more broadly across the public and private sectors attempt with Cloud Service implementation.

The critical change needed rests with public and private sector entities identifying third-party auditors knowledgeable about the overall process and the specific control satisfaction elements. Secure Agile Cybersecurity is possible.

A Need for Third-Party Assessment

A significant challenge for the NIST-based framework is the **fox-watching-the-hen-house** issue. While RMF allows for self-assessment and self-scoring of a company or agency's control posture, it has proven an ongoing problem in every corner of the government and private sector. The lack of independent third-party assessments is the greatest danger to a real long-term solution to proper security; Risk Management as a critical principle has failed in securing IT environments at no fault of its own. The NIST control approach has been the most significant contribution to cybersecurity; however, the dysfunction occurs when agencies and companies implement such control-based solutions without a clear and focused understanding of what it truly needs to meet a secure state.

It is strongly recommended that a third-party, NIST-based security audit agency ensures control compliance. The company, agency, or organization must also mandate and seek a third-party auditing agency to confirm that the controls are correctly implemented. The total costs of such auditors are as much as $300,000. More typically, the price will be in the $150,000 to $200,000 range. Our strongest advice remains; do **_NOT_** assess your cybersecurity posture; the costs paid up-front will ensure reduced liability if the companies data is lost, compromised, or destroyed.

The Subjectivity of Compliance

Ultimately, how to best apply the secure agile frameworks is left to the implementing company or agency. The cybersecurity professional, either as part of the development or system operational maintenance support element, will essentially assist the system owner in making a subjective determination of which controls will be applied and to what degree makes sense based upon the expected threats and risks to the system. The respective frameworks are a living collection of security documents and will be updated by security professionals. The federal government will drive any future addition or expansion as they focus on the criticality of cyber-protection needs for the nation.

Furthermore, the "critical infrastructure community" will be the most impacted by any changes. This will include public and private owners and other bodies with a specific role in securing the national infrastructure. Members of the critical infrastructure community perform functions that are supported by the broad category of cybersecurity.[6]

To manage cybersecurity risks, a clear understanding of the organization's business drivers and security considerations specific to its use of technology is required. Because each organization's risks, priorities, and systems are unique, the tools and methods used to achieve the outcomes described will vary. This book is focused on a diligent and honest self-assessment by the company or agency—where that is not done, the cyber-posture of any IT environment will have varying states of risk. *An honest effort is essential to pursue secure and agile system development as a formula for IT and data security protections.*

In the case of the NCF, it is an effective model because it is technology-neutral. The strength of NCF, while it establishes necessary standards, guidelines, and best practices, it does not mandate any form of technology to meet a control. This book further suggests several market solutions, but they are only used in the historical use of such products.[7]

By relying on such standards, guidelines, and practices, the NCF is an ideal model for effective cyber-protections. The use of existing and emerging standards will enable economies of scale and drive the development of secure and effective products, services, and practices that meet identified industry needs and requirements. This overall leads to secure system development so desperately needed.

Additionally, leveraging NCF as a guideline of standard taxonomies and mechanisms for organizations supports the following through an effective and managed cybersecurity lifecycle. It includes:

- **Define the current cybersecurity posture**
- **Define objective state for cybersecurity**

---

[6] The former term was "Information Assurance" and may be more accurate while "cybersecurity" has wide-ranging interpretations that will continue to add especially some confusion with external stakeholders.
[7] Registered or trademarked products identified are only discussed as examples; there is no intent to solicit a single solution; these are the only solutions to the respective technical needs to meet an NCF control.

- Classify and prioritize opportunities for improvement, which includes a continuous and repeatable process
- Measure progress toward the objective state
- Communicate with internal and external stakeholders about cybersecurity threats, risk, and tolerances

The NCF complements and does not replace an organization's risk management process and cybersecurity program. The organization can use its current processes and leverage the NCF to identify opportunities to strengthen and communicate its management of cybersecurity risk while aligning with industry practices. Alternatively, an organization without an existing cybersecurity program can use the NCF as a reference to establish one.

While the NCF has been developed to improve cybersecurity risk management related to critical infrastructure, organizations can use it in any sector of the economy or society. It is intended to be helpful to companies, government agencies, and not-for-profit organizations regardless of their focus or size. The common taxonomy of standards, guidelines and practices that it provides also is not country-specific. Organizations outside the United States may also use the NCF to strengthen their cybersecurity efforts. The NCF can contribute to developing a common language for international cooperation on critical infrastructure cybersecurity.

National Institute of Standards and Technology 800-171

We have included a NIST 800-171 Compliance Checklist with all functional security controls to include the recently released and more granular controls of NIST 800-171A at Appendix G

Where is 800-171 Going?

In late 2018, the expectation is that the US federal government will expand the NIST Special Publication (SP) 800-171, revision 1, ***Protecting Unclassified Information in Nonfederal Information Systems and Organizations*** cybersecurity technical publication will apply to the entirety of the government and any company providing goods or services to the federal government. It will require that any company, business, or agency supporting the US Government be fully compliant with NIST 800-171 no later than the contract award date.

The Federal Acquisition Regulation (FAR) Committee's Case # 2017-016 had an original suspense date of March 2018; that date has come and gone. The latest and expected timeframe for any final decision has moved to a scheduled timeframe of November 2018. While the Federal Acquisition Regulation (FAR) Committee may further delay NIST 800-171 implementation, this book's value and purpose are no less critical.

This chapter is created to help small and big business owners in meeting the newest cybersecurity contracting requirement. It is intended to assist companies and their IT staff in best addressing the challenges of meeting the 2016 NIST 800-171, revision 1. This further includes compliance with the FAR clause 52.204-21 and its companion DOD supplement, the Defense Federal Acquisition Regulation Supplement (DFARS), and its specific clause, 252.204-7012.

NIST 800-171 is expected to apply to **prime and subcontractors** alike. There are three core contractual obligations:

1. "Adequately safeguard" Controlled Unclassified Information (CUI), and if working with the Department of Defense (DOD), Covered/Critical Defense Information (CDI).

2. Provide timely cyber-incident reporting to the government when an IT network breach is identified; typically, within 72 hours or sooner.

3. If operating with a Cloud Service Provider (CSP), "adequate" security needs to be demonstrated; usually, a contract with the CSP shows that they are providing adequate security to provide data protection as a third-party service provider. A contract or Service Level Agreement (SLA) should reveal the business is executing sound cybersecurity diligence to government Contract Officers (CO).

What is "adequate security?" **Adequate security** is defined by "compliance" with the 110 NIST 800-171 security controls and when the business is issued the solicitation, i.e., contract award. It will also be considered adequate upon an authorization issued to the business or company by the designated CO. This does not mean all security controls are in effect. Still, where a deviation is needed, the company or agency provides a Plan of Action and Milestones (POAM).

A POAM is required as part of the official submission package to the government. (See the supplementary guide: Writing an Effective Plan of Action & Milestones (POAM) available on Amazon®.) It should identify why the company cannot currently address the control and when it expects to resolve it.

The business must also provide timely cyber-incident reporting to the government when a breach of its network has occurred. The DOD requirement, for example, is that the business notifies the government within 72 hours upon *recognition* of a security incident. (See the chapter on the Incident Response (IR) control family).

Additionally, the US Government may require the business to notify cybersecurity support and response elements within the federal government. This may include the Department of Homeland Security's (DHS) US Computer Emergency Response Team (US-CERT) (https://www.us-cert.gov/) or other like an agency within the government.

Changing federal cybersecurity contract requirements also considers the vast moves within the public and private sectors into cloud services. Typically, the security protections would be found in any contracts or SLA between the business and the CSP. These are usually enough evidence for the government.

The good news regarding CSPs is that many current CSPs are already in compliance with the government's Federal Risk and Authorization Management Program (FedRAMP). Being FEDRAMP-compliant before final submission of the NIST 800-171 Body of Evidence (BOE) will reduce the challenges of using an uncertified CSP; plan accordingly if considering moving part or all the business' operations into the "cloud."

Consequences of Non-compliance

There are several significant consequences contractors and subcontractors need to consider if they cannot meet or maintain their compliance. This can include several severe consequences, and the business must stay current regarding any changes in its cybersecurity posture. Stay constantly present regarding any new NIST 800-171 direction in general or specific to the agency being supported. Failing to stay current with the Contract office may jeopardize business relationships with the government. These consequences may include:

- Impact on Future Contract Selection. This may be as basic as a temporary disbarment from federal contract work. It could also include permanent measures by the government to suspend a company for a much more extended period. Furthermore, the government could pursue the company for fraud or clear misrepresentation of their security posture to the US Government. This most likely would occur when a cybersecurity **incident** occurs within the businesses' network. This most likely would result in a government-appointed third-party assessor determining whether there was a willful disregard for NIST 800-171 and any associated FAR/DFARS clauses. *Remember*, the business will continually be assessed against the following criteria:

- o Was there **adequate security** in place before and during the incident?
- o Were the protections adequately established based upon a **good-faith** effort by the company to protect CUI/CDI?

- <u>Assessments Initiated by the Government.</u> At this phase, the Government will have unfettered access to determine the culpability of the incident and whether it further brought harm against the government and its agencies. Cooperation is a crucial obligation, and hiding the incident may have worse impacts than not reporting the intrusion.

- <u>A POAM will be required.</u> The government will most likely mandate a POAM be developed to address the finding. This should be an excellent effort to identify interim milestones with final and planned completion dates to ensure a situation will not reoccur. (See the supplement: *Writing an Effective Plan of Action & Milestones:* https://www.amazon.com/Writing-Effective-Plan-Action-Milestones/dp/1720176558/ref=tmm_pap_swatch_0?_encoding=UTF8&qid=1542058383&sr=8-1-fkmr0).

- <u>Loss of Contract.</u> Worse case, the Contract Officer may determine that the company failed to meet the cybersecurity requirements. The results of that determination most likely will result in the cancelation of the contract for cause.

The Likely Course: FAR Clause 52.204-21

For <u>fundamental</u> safeguarding of contractor information systems that process, store, or transmit federal "contract information," expect this clause will be modified to reduce several of the specific NIST 800-171 security controls. A pared-down selection of controls would be used in the early stages of a federal agency's NIST 800-171 implementation and transition. FAR 52.204-21 may be modified to fifteen (15) "basic" cybersecurity controls for the contractor's information system. This will typically apply to "federal contract information," where a company stores, processes, or transmits federal data. The specific language is:

> *"Information, not intended for public release, that is provided by or generated for the Government under a contract to develop or deliver a product or service to the Government, but not including information provided to the public (such as on public Web sites) or simple transactional information, such as necessary to process payments."*

This clause will <u>not</u> require all 110 security controls and is expected to reduce or minimize the following types of associated controls:

1) Cybersecurity training requirements
2) Two-factor authentication (2FA)
3) Detailed system control descriptions
4) Cybersecurity incidents or breach notifications

Expect few federal agencies to apply this clause long-term since it opens the federal agency to public and congressional scrutiny. Expect this to be used as a short-term solution until such time a future contract modification occurs, and the agency is more confident in its understanding and application of NIST 800-171.

Finally, this chapter is still applicable for the FAR 52.204-21 implementation scenario. It can answer the expected 15 security controls as identified in subsequent chapters of this book. Verify the required security controls with the Contract Office. It is crucial to confirm the needed control explanations as described later in the specified in later chapters and their respective control family.

Proof of a company's cybersecurity posture

The basis of NIST 800-171 is that contractors provide adequate security on all covered contractor Information Systems (IS). Typically, the minimum requirement to demonstrate control implementation is through **documentation**. Another term that is used throughout this book is an **artifact**. An artifact is any representation to a Contract Office or independent third-party assessor that shows compliance with specific security controls. It is a significant part of the proof that a business owner would provide to the federal government.

The common term for collecting all applications and supporting artifacts is the Body of Evidence (BOE). The essential items required for the BOE includes three major items:

1. **Company Policy or Procedure.** For this book, these terms are used interchangeably. Essentially any direction provided to internal employees and subcontractors is enforceable under US labor laws and Human Resource (HR) direction. It is recommended that such a policy or procedure artifact be a unique collection of how the company addresses 110 security controls.

> *All cybersecurity-related policy or procedure requirements are best captured in a single business policy or procedure guide. This should address the controls aligned with the security control families*

2. **System Security Plan (SSP).** This is a standard cybersecurity document. It describes the company's overall IT infrastructure to include hardware and software lists. Where appropriate, suggestions of additional artifacts that should be included in this document and duplicated into a standard SSP format will be recommended. (See *System Security Plan (SSP) Template and Workbook: A Supplement to "DOD NIST 800-171 Compliance Guidebook* "on Amazon®)

A *free* 36-minute introduction to the SSP is currently available on Udemy.com at https://www.udemy.com/system-security-plan-ssp-for-nist-800-171-compliance/.

3. **Plans of Action and Milestones (POAM).** This describes any control that the company cannot fix or fully demonstrate its full compliance. It provides an opportunity for a company to delay addressing a difficulty implement a technical solution or because the cost may be prohibitive.

POAMs should always have an expected completion date and defined interim milestones that describe the actions leading to a full resolution or implementation of the control. *POAMs typically should not be for more than a year; however, a critical hint, a company can request an <u>extension</u> multiple times if unable to fully meet the control.*

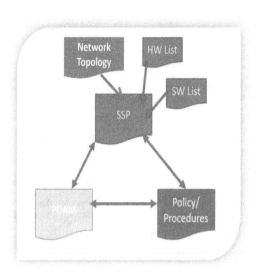

The Major Artifacts Required by the Federal Government under NIST 800-171

NIST 800-171 is the second current agile solution already being used and administered in parts of the federal government and is already a requirement within the DOD. The expectation still affords the likelihood that this will become contractually mandatory across the federal government in late 2018. It provides its own constrained amount of controls that support agility. NIST 800-171 is likely to be a wide-ranging standard and supports the goals of rapid functional and security updates in a more complex and threatening cyberspace arena.

The Risk Assessment (RA)

The RA Defined

A change to a system may introduce new vulnerabilities or may interfere with existing security controls. An impact analysis should be conducted before system modifications to determine if there will be a significant impact to the system security posture caused by the changes; this effort may be described as a security impact assessment, but the output of this effort always results in a documented RA. If the analysis reveals that there will be a significant impact if the proposed change is made, then additional research or testing of the modification may be required, or a security reauthorization may be warranted. If the changes do not significantly impact the security status, then the changes should still be assessed (e.g., tested) before moving to production. Continuous monitoring and testing should be executed to monitor and control any adverse effects on the system.

The general steps of the risk or security impact analysis are as follows:
- Understand the change in a system change request
- Identify vulnerabilities that the proposed change may introduce
- Assess risks to the information system, system users, and the organization's mission/business functions
- Assess security controls that are impacted by the proposed change; for instance, there may be a cascade effect or interference on other security controls
- Plan safeguards and countermeasures to the identified impacts
- Update critical security documentation to reflect the changes made to the information system.

When continuous monitoring identifies a potential problem that needs to be examined (for example, an Intrusion Prevention System (IPS) detects an attempted change to a data stream not defined in a threat signature database), the following items should be considered:

- Identify impacts on other security controls that the problem may be causing.
- Identify any inconsistencies between security policies, procedures, and IT practices that the problem may have uncovered.

If such an examination indicates that a change must be made to the system, the risk analysis steps above should be followed. Once the analysis has validated the need for a change, the system owner may consider doing the following actions:

1. *Determine the risk level of making the change*
2. *Identify the cost of an incident if a threat actor exploited the vulnerability*
3. *Identify the cost of mitigating a vulnerability*

4. *Identify any compensatory or mitigating controls that may enhance or augment the specified control*

The results obtained during continuous monitoring activities should consider any necessary updates to the SSP and the POAM. Since the Authorizing Official, Information System Owner, and Security Control Auditor (Assessor) will be using these items to guide future security assessment activities, they must be as complete as possible; incomplete documentation may result in disapproval of the approved change.

After the assessment, tentative changes to the system should be formulated and a Risk Analysis performed. An RA should be undertaken if uncertain modifications or other changes (e.g., compensating controls) are implemented. Risk will be assessed for each issue identified from continuous monitoring. An organization-defined procedure will track each discovered deficiency or vulnerability (e.g., using a tool or approach that documents whether the item is open or closed, how it was resolved when it was resolved, and whether it required a POAM entry). The Information System Security Officer (ISSO) and Authorizing Official (or Authorizing Official Designated Representative) will acknowledge a review and approval of the issues resolved. This should also include any open issues and how the system owner or developer is tracking them.

The RA Workflow

The RA is the *greatest* tool to bring agility into any IT environment. Once the system is deployed, there are typically regular system functionality changes requested or required to meet the operational demands of the organization. Most will have a "positive" effect on the state of its cybersecurity posture, and some will not. Either of these changes requires that a RA be accomplished. An RA "bridges" both the agile and non-agile frameworks in existence. For example, the Defense Health Agency (DHA) in Falls Church, Virginia, has been an expert in this area for years. The diagram below provides a revolutionary workflow around the principle of "security relevance." It provides an innovative model for the cybersecurity community.

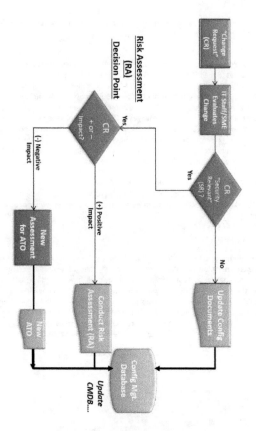

Decision-tree Addressing "Security Relevance"

1. The process begins when the developer identifies a needed change to the existing and accredited baseline. As part of that process, a "Change Request" (CR) will be generated, and associated Configuration Management (CM) reviews will occur, including a determination of **Security Relevance (SR)**.

"Security Relevance"

All hardware and software changes will be evaluated whether they are security-relevant. Security relevant is defined as "Any change to a system's configuration, environment, information content, functionality, or users which have the potential to change the risk imposed upon its continued operations, (Committee on National Security Systems Instruction (CNSSI)-4009)."

---

2. Suppose it is determined that the change will alter the system's hardware, software, or architecture components. In that case, a full ATO effort may be required—a complete revalidation of the previous chosen Agile Framework will be required, and the process will have to be re-executed.

3. If it is determined there is a "minor" and frequent change to the baseline. Then an abbreviated RA may accompany the CR and be forwarded to the appropriate decision-maker/System Owner (SO) for resolution. It will be submitted to the decision-maker for review and final approval in this case.

4. Suppose it is determined this is a "major" and "security-relevant" change to the baseline. In that case, an RA with an associated Risk Analysis will accompany the CR and forwarded to the SO for approval based upon the security engineer's recommendation. Typically, an Information Systems Security Engineer (ISSE) will prepare the RA (See Appendix D as an example report format) and forwarded it to company decision-makers for concurrence/approval. Assuming a concurrence, the RA will be submitted to the SO for final review and the to an Authorizing Official (AO) per NIST guidance for final approval.

5. Once approved, the information packet will be placed in a designated repository such as the CM database. The CM database provides the system, program, etc., a record repository for future review or audit purposes; the CM database is a required security control element.

The RA and Agility

An RA is intended to "streamline" the RMF Assessment and Authorization (A&A) process for changes within the system's baseline. It is intended to reduce the overall need to accomplish a "full" ATO activity, and it leverages this **security control** to reduce program volatility. An RA will be used instead of an ATO effort when no security-relevant changes negatively impact the baseline[8]. Configuration updates to the baseline to correct approved functional capabilities as part of the operational support to the user do not require a complete ATO effort.

A Risk Assessment Report (RAR) is required throughout the life of the system. It is not the same as the RA but is the foundational guide that provides information and intelligence about internal and external risks to the system. It will be updated as risks, and threats change against the system. This will include version or build changes that occur during the normal process of maintaining and enhancing the readiness of the system to meet customer requirements; this does not have to be version changes.

While the NIST 800-171 is a strategic approach to agile, the RA is a tactical implementation. We have included in Appendix D examples of a Risk Analysis submission report. The RA is the most flexible and substantive low-level solution to help integrate into an effective, secure, agile environment. Additionally, The RA is a significantly underutilized capability but can be a specific solution to keeping pace with agile development efforts.

---

[8] While not typical, using a less-capable firewall that does not support, for example, white-listing would result in a weaker state of security.

Specialized IT Systems (SPITS)

Constrained Number of Controls

This discussion on an emerging cybersecurity tactical approach to injecting even a lower-level RA process into existing NIST-based frameworks. The **SPecialized Information Technology System (SPITS)** is designed to afford additional agile-like solutions for singular purposed IT systems. These would include "plug-and-play" systems running on some form of computer architecture with some form of Operating System (OS) or even firmware. This could also include Systems on a Chip (SOC) such as Field Programmable Gate Arrays (FPGA) and Application Specific Integrated Circuits (ASIC). Examples would consist of test systems to determine calibration levels of other devices and sensors on a Major IT System (MITS)[9], administrative consoles to collect audit logs for analysis and forensic activities, add-on modules such as Global Positioning Systems (GPS) to provide location information to a primary IT system. Such systems may be integrated with the central IT system or connect on an intermittent basis—the longer-term connections would require future updates to the significant systems overall architecture and require updates to the System Security Plan (SSP) at a minimum.

Examples may include:

- "Plug and play" or applique IT solutions intended to increase the functionality of the overall system
- Test devices and tools
- Administrative and maintenance computers (consoles)

SPITS would also include operating software, applications, etc., and their associated hardware to include embedded computer systems which enable that system to perform their interactive tasks with Major IT System (MITS)[10]. It may also be a special-purpose component, to include systems and their associated hardware, software, and firmware; this could have, for example, onboard video collection devices or other single-purpose IT system which provides specialized processing activities within the MITS's security boundary; it is not necessary to provide security controls to a device/module supplied from a "trusted" source with requisite certification(s) affirming it has been processed through an approved security process, e.g., National Information Assurance Partnership (NIAP). See its website to review current systems at https://www.niap-ccevs.org/.

---

[9] A MITS is defined as the main system providing security controls inherited by other "tethered" IT systems to include SPITS that are typically of a singular functional purpose, e.g., full-motion camera, GPS, etc.
[10] It is expected numerous controls will be inherited from the MITS allowing for agile integration and adequate security control implementation.

For the purposes of SPITS use, we have further leveraged the NIST 800-53 revision 4, "Security and Privacy Controls for Federal Information Systems and Organization"[11] cybersecurity directive for federal organizations. We have done this because it provides a much finer listing of technical controls required to make these single-function systems "cyber-secure." We have chosen controls at the software coding review and assessment levels and above as defined within NIST 800-53.

The proposed controls are currently restricted to 9 controls. This defined number of controls further supports an agile-like mechanism to assist in secure system development. These controls are under consideration by many cybersecurity professionals within the Cybersecurity Community, but there has been no formal adoption of them as a matter of standard.

The listing below provides the beginnings of a mini-framework ideal for IT sub-system cybersecurity protections. A full description of the controls with recommended actions and periodicity may be found in Appendix F: "Special Information Technology Systems Baseline Controls." They are:

1. **RA-3: Risk Assessment**
2. **RA-5: Vulnerability Scanning**
3. **CM-6: Document Configuration Settings**
4. **SA-11: Security Testing and Evaluation**
5. **SA-12 Supply Chain Protection**
6. **SI-2: Flaw Remediation**
7. **SI-11 Error Handling**
8. **SI-16 Memory Protection**
9. **SC-8 Transmission Confidentiality and Integrity**

SPITS Categorization

SPITS has three (3) significant sub-system categories based upon the physical location and permanence (temporal relationship) to a MITS. They are:

1. **CATEGORY 1:** INTEGRATED/EMBEDDED SUB-SYSTEM
   a. Description: This is an IT-based subsystem providing additional functionality or capabilities to the MITS. It becomes part of the designated security boundary once approved by the System Owner/Authorizing Official. There is no intent to remove except under extreme circumstances or upon identifying a significant security vulnerability that cannot be addressed.
   b. Permanence: Permanent

---

[11] A DRAFT NIST 800-53 revision 5 was released in August 2017; its authorized implementation for the federal government has yet to be announced.

      c. Examples: Video collection/capture device; GPS; anti-tamper monitoring device; additional firewalls; "black box" archival device.

2. **CATEGORY 2:** APPLIQUE SUB-SYSTEM
    a. Description: This is an IT device physically connecting to external ports of the MITS. It becomes part of the security boundary once approved by the SO/AO.
    b. Permanence: May be permanent or non-permanent based upon mission needs and requirements.
    c. Examples: "Strap-on" guidance system to a "dumb bomb;" digital radio; externally mounted camera.

3. **CATEGORY 3:** INTERMITTENT (TEMPORARY) SUB-SYSTEM
    a. Description: This is an IT device that only touches the security boundary for a limited period. It is not intended to be a permanent connection to the MITS.
    b. Permanence: Non-permanent.
    c. Examples: maintenance or audit (forensic) collection computer; calibration device; test device to ascertain functionality, accuracy, reliability, etc.

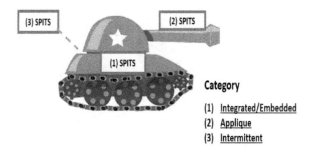

Three Categories of Specialized IT Systems (SPITS)

SPITS is a mini-framework and is currently only being considered in specific sectors of the US federal government. It has not yet been formally adopted. This concept within this publication intends to begin a discussion with the release of this book. The desire is to create agile tools, methodologies, and solutions that afford IT developers greater and more secure systems.

Conclusion

NCF is proving to be another success story for many who believed the NCF framework might be too hard to implement. When you work in the field of cybersecurity, for example, such as NIST 800-53 revision 4 you realize that 400-800 security controls are a problematic endeavor even for the cybersecurity developer, auditor, or assessor to effectively understand and manage in the ever-changing posed by national and international hackers and nation-state threats. With the advent of NIST 800-171and the NCF, it creates a finite number that is easier to manage and assess. It has proven successful in many areas such as private companies and academic institutions; it no longer seems daunting for the business or cybersecurity "sentinel" to stop the threats "in their tracks."

The NCF has proven to be successful to include the University of Chicago Biological Sciences Division (BSD). Their Chief Information Security Officer, Plamen Martinov, stated: "there are many security frameworks, but we found that the [National] Cybersecurity Framework was well-aligned with our main objective, which was to establish a common language for communicating cybersecurity risks across the Division." NCF provides the common language to allow for connection and reciprocity[12] assurances when connecting to other networks.

They implemented BSD, and their consultants established a team of cybersecurity engineers, subject matter experts, and security analysts to implement the NCF. The team used a combination of risk management and NCF principles to develop four phases, including a Current State, Assessment, Target State, and Roadmap phases. During Phase 1, *Current State*, the team reviewed existing policies and practices to define the state of BSD's cybersecurity program. In Phase 2, the team conducted an in-depth risk assessment across all its departments. The team defined risk thresholds and the desired target state for BSD's cybersecurity program in Phase 3. They aligned their policies, procedures, and practices to the NCF controls (subcategories) during the Target phase. Finally, the team concluded the project in Phase 4 by developing a prioritized roadmap that outlined the activities required for the departments within BSD to achieve the target state.

Some of their benefits **include:**

- **Aligned security risk expectations** across all 23 departments through a risk register aligned to the NCF
- Identified security requirements as a **standard set of target outcomes** while enabling departments to define the approach for achieving their outcomes

---

[12] "Reciprocity" is the principle of accepting connections to another network or networks based upon an agreed to security framework. Where there is commonality of terms and standards it ensures that each system owner has the confidence that other networks are meeting the same and stringent protections afforded by a widely accepted standard such as the NCF.

- **Prioritized security goals** across the division within a resourced roadmap outlining security gap concluding activities

After implementing NCF, BSD trained all of its users on the security program and continually monitored improvements. Several key initiatives were begun to implement enterprise-wide cybersecurity capabilities to meet their objective goals to secure their IT environment.

For example, the NCF has proven to be an employable model for securing critical infrastructure across the US and potentially around the globe. It has a defined and manageable set of controls, and it removes the complexities and dangers of incomplete or unmet security controls. No matter the opinion, the classic RMF process based on NIST 800-53 has been less than a success story. Specifically, NCF and NIST 800-171 at the strategic level have proven to be the right approach and model that keeps the cybersecurity professional's challenge of meeting security to a manageable level, a level that assures better protections.

The RA and the SPITS will contribute to agile development at the more tactical level as they are better understood and employed. The RA has always been a *jack-rabbit* solution that has always been a part of NIST-based frameworks. The SPITS model affords an innovative solution that can be used today; this plug-and-play and focused nine security controls can protect an overall MITS either in the public or private sectors. These tactical approaches will provide much-needed mechanisms to comport with the demands of agile.

Driven by even more network intrusions into the wide range of private and public-sector entities, these solutions exist today. They will form the foundation of securing our national critical infrastructures. Furthermore, the functional and security developer world must integrate far better by leveraging the A/SDLC with the proposed frameworks and approaches needed to secure vital networks and data globally.

It will require the role of system owners, developers, cybersecurity professionals, and specialists with a keen understanding of such defensive measures that will ensure the best protection to the nation's respective security boundaries, companies, and agencies. The front line of defense rests with these experts to bring such cybersecurity best practices and procedures to the nation. These will help reduce and eliminate the threats as they continue to intrude into networks nationally and worldwide.

SECTION 4: APPENDICES

Appendix A—Relevant Terms

Audit log.
A chronological record of information system activities, including records of system accesses and operations performed in each period.

Authentication.
Verifying the identity of a user, process, or device, often a prerequisite to allowing access to resources in an information system.

Availability.
Ensuring timely and reliable access to and use of information.

Baseline Configuration.
A documented set of specifications for an information system, or a configuration item within a system, has been formally reviewed and agreed on at a given point in time, which can be changed only through change control procedures.

Blacklisting.
The process used to identify: (i) software programs that are not authorized to execute on an information system; or (ii) prohibited websites.

Confidentiality.
Preserving authorized restrictions on information access and disclosure, including means for protecting personal privacy and proprietary information.

Configuration Management. A collection of activities focused on establishing and maintaining the integrity of information technology products and information systems through control of processes for initializing, changing, and monitoring the configurations of those products and systems throughout the system development life cycle.

Controlled Unclassified Information (CUI/CDI). Information that law, regulation, or governmentwide policy requires has safeguarding or disseminating controls, excluding information classified under Executive Order 13526, Classified National Security Information, December 29, 2009, any predecessor or successor order, or the Atomic Energy Act of 1954, as amended.

Cybersecurity
The process of protecting information by preventing, detecting, and responding to attacks.

Cybersecurity Event   A cybersecurity change that ***may*** impact organizational operations (including mission, capabilities, or reputation).

Cybersecurity Incident A cybersecurity event determined to impact the organization prompting the need for response and recovery.

External network.   A network not controlled by the company.

FIPS-validated cryptography.   The Cryptographic Module Validation Program (CMVP) validated a cryptographic module to meet requirements specified in FIPS Publication 140-2 (as amended). As a prerequisite to CMVP validation, the cryptographic module must implement a cryptographic algorithm that has successfully passed validation testing by the Cryptographic Algorithm Validation Program (CAVP).

Hardware.   The physical components of an information system.

Incident.   An occurrence that actually or potentially jeopardizes the confidentiality, integrity, or availability of an information system or the information the system processes, stores, or transmits or constitutes a violation or imminent threat of a breach of security policies, security procedures, or acceptable use policies.

Information Security.   Protecting information and information systems from unauthorized access, use, disclosure, disruption, modification, or destruction to provide confidentiality, integrity, and availability.

Information System.   A discrete set of information resources is organized for collecting, processing, maintenance, use, sharing, dissemination, or disposition of information.

Information Technology. Any equipment or interconnected system or subsystem of equipment used in the automatic acquisition, storage, manipulation, management, movement, control, display, switching, interchange, transmission, or reception of data or information by the executive agency. It includes computers, ancillary equipment, software, firmware, and similar procedures, services (including support services), and related resources.

Integrity.   Guarding against improper information modification or destruction and includes ensuring information non-repudiation and authenticity.

Internal Network. A network where: (i) the establishment, maintenance, and provisioning of security controls are under the direct control of organizational employees or contractors; or (ii) cryptographic encapsulation or similar security technology implemented between organization-controlled endpoints provides the same effect (at least about confidentiality and integrity).

Malicious Code. Software intended to perform an unauthorized process that will adversely impact an information system's confidentiality, integrity, or availability. A virus, worm, Trojan horse, or other code-based entity that infects a host. Spyware and some forms of adware are also examples of malicious code.

Media. Physical devices or writing surfaces include magnetic tapes, optical disks, magnetic disks, and printouts (including display media) onto which information is recorded, stored, or printed within an information system.

Mobile Code. Software programs or parts of programs obtained from remote information systems, transmitted across a network, and executed on a local information system without explicit installation or execution by the recipient.

Mobile device. A portable computing device that: (i) has a small form factor such that a single individual can easily carry it; (ii) is designed to operate without a physical connection (e.g., wirelessly transmit or receive information); (iii) possesses local, nonremovable or removable data storage; and (iv) includes a self-contained power source. Mobile devices may also include voice communication capabilities, onboard sensors that allow the devices to capture information, and/or built-in features for synchronizing local data with remote locations. Examples include smartphones, tablets, and E-readers.

Multifactor Authentication. Authentication using two or more different factors to achieve authentication. Factors include: (i) something you know (e.g., password/PIN); (ii) something you have (e.g., cryptographic identification device, token); or (iii) something you are (e.g., biometric).

Nonfederal Information System. An information system that does not meet the criteria for a federal information system. Nonfederal organization.

Network. Information system(s) implemented with a collection of interconnected components. Such components may include routers, hubs, cabling, telecommunications controllers, key distribution centers, and technical control devices.

Portable storage device. An information system component that can be inserted into and removed from an information system is used to store data or information (e.g., text, video, audio, and/or image data). Such components are typically implemented on magnetic, optical, or solid-state devices (e.g., floppy disks, compact/digital video disks, flash/thumb drives, external hard disk drives, and flash memory cards/drives containing nonvolatile memory).

Privileged Account. An information system account with authorizations of a privileged user.

Privileged User. A user that is authorized (and therefore, trusted) to perform security-relevant functions that ordinary users are not authorized to perform.

Remote Access. Access to an organizational information system by a user (or a process acting on behalf of a user) communicating through an external network (e.g., the Internet).

Risk. A measure of the extent to which a potential circumstance or event threatens an entity, and typically a function of (i) the adverse impacts that would arise if the circumstance or event occurs; and (ii) the likelihood of occurrence. Information system-related security risks are those risks that arise from the loss of confidentiality, integrity, or availability of information or information systems and reflect the potential adverse impacts to organizational operations (including mission, functions, image, or reputation), organizational assets, individuals, other organizations, and the Nation.

Sanitization. Actions taken to render data written on media unrecoverable by both ordinary and, for some forms of sanitization, extraordinary means. The process to remove information from media such that data recovery is not possible. It includes removing all classified labels, markings, and activity logs.

Security Control. A safeguard or countermeasure is prescribed for an information system or organization designed to protect its information's confidentiality, integrity, and availability and meet a set of defined security requirements.

Security Control Assessment.   The testing or evaluation of security controls to determine the extent to which the controls are implemented correctly, operating as intended and producing the desired

Security Functions.   The hardware, software, and/or firmware of the information system is responsible for enforcing the system security policy and supporting the isolation of code and data on which the protection is based.

Threat.   Any circumstance or event with the potential to adversely impact organizational operations (including mission, functions, image, or reputation), organizational assets, individuals, other organizations, or the Nation through an information system via unauthorized access, destruction, disclosure, modification of information, and/or denial of service.

Whitelisting.   The process used to identify: (i) software programs that are authorized to execute on an information system.

Defining Continuous Monitoring

Cybersecurity is not about shortcuts. There are no easy solutions to years of leaders demurring their responsibility to address the growing threats in cyberspace. Several years ago, we hoped that the Office of Personnel Management (OPM) breach would herald the needed focus, energy, and funding to quash the bad guys. That has proven an empty hope where leaders have abrogated their responsibility to lead in cyberspace. The "holy grail" solution of Continuous Monitoring (ConMon) has been the most misunderstood solution where too many shortcuts are perpetrated by numerous federal agencies and the private sector to create an illusion of success. This paper is specifically written to help leaders better understand what constitutes an accurate statement of: "we have continuous monitoring." This is not about shortcuts. This is about education, training, and understanding that cybersecurity is not a technical but a leadership issue at the highest leadership levels.

The Committee on National Security Systems defines ConMon as: "[t]he processes implemented to maintain current security status for one or more information systems on which the operational mission of the enterprise depends" (CNSS, 2010). ConMon has been described as the holistic solution of end-to-end cybersecurity coverage and the answer to providing an effective global Risk Management (RM) solution. It promises the elimination of the 3-year recertification cycle that has been the bane of cybersecurity professionals.

For ConMon to become a reality for any agency, it must meet the measures and expectations defined in the National Institute of Standards and Technology (NIST) Special Publication (SP) 800-137, Information Security Continuous Monitoring for Federal Information Systems and Organizations. "Continuous monitoring has evolved as a best practice for managing risk on an ongoing basis" (SANS Institute, 2016); it is an instrument that supports effective, continual, and recurring RM assurances. For any agency to espouse it to attain full ConMon compliance, it must coordinate all the described significant elements found in NIST SP 800-137.

ConMon is not just the passive visibility piece but also includes the active efforts of vulnerability scanning, threat alert, reduction, mitigation, or elimination of a dynamic Information Technology (IT) environment. The Department of Homeland Security (DHS) has couched its approach to ConMon more holistically. Their program to protect government networks is more aptly called: "Continuous Diagnostics and Monitoring" or CDM and includes a need to react to an active network attacker. "The ability to make IT networks, end-points, and applications visible; to identify malicious activity; and to respond [emphasis added] immediately is critical to defending information systems and networks" (Sann, 2016).

Another description of ConMon can be found in NIST's CAESARS Framework Extension: An Enterprise Continuous Monitoring Technical Reference Model (Second Draft). It defines its essential characteristics within the concept of "Continuous Security Monitoring." It is described as a "...risk management approach to Cybersecurity that maintains a picture of an organization's security posture, provides visibility into assets, leverages the use of automated data feeds, monitors the effectiveness of security controls, and enables prioritization of remedies," (NIST, 2012); it must demonstrate visibility, data feeds, measures of effectiveness and allow for solutions. It provides another description of what should be presented to ensure full ConMon designation under the NIST standard.

The government's Federal Risk and Authorization Management Program (Fed-RAMP) has defined similar ConMon goals. These objectives are all key outcomes of a successful ConMon implementation. Its "... goal[s]...[are] to provide: (i) operational visibility; (ii) annual self-attestations on security control implementations; (iii) managed change control; (iv) and attendance to incident response duties," (GSA, 2012). While not explicit to NIST SP 800-37, these objectives are well-aligned with the desires of an effective and complete solution.

RMF creates the structure and documentation needs of ConMon; it represents the specific implementation and oversight of Information Security (IS) within an IT environment. It supports the general activity of RM within an agency. (See Figure 1 below). The RMF "... describes a disciplined and structured process that integrates information security and risk management activities into the system development life cycle" (NIST-B, 2011). RMF is the structure that both describes and relies upon ConMon as its risk oversight and effective mechanism between IS and RM.

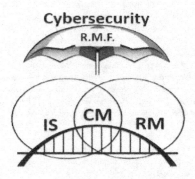

Figure 1. CM "bridges" Information Security and Risk Management

This article provides a conceptual framework to address how an agency identifies a proper ConMon solution through NIST SP 800-137. It discusses the additional need to align component requirements with the *"11 Security Automation Domains"* necessary to implement true ConMon. (See Figure 2 below). It is through the complete implementation and

Figure 2. The 11 Security Automation Domains (NIST, 2011)

integration with the other described components—See Figure 3 below--that an organization can correctly state it has achieved ConMon.

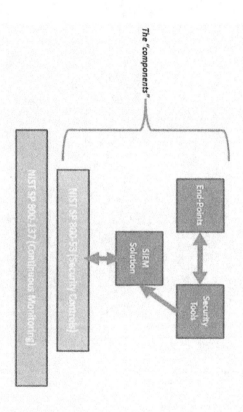

Figure 3. The "Components" of an Effective Continuous Monitoring

Continuous Monitoring – First Generation

For ConMon to be effective and genuine, it must align end-point visibility with security monitoring tools. This includes security monitoring tools with connectivity to "end-points" such as laptops, desktops, servers, routers, firewalls, etc. Additionally, these must work with a highly integrated Security Information and Event Management (SIEM) device. The other "component" is a clear linkage between the end-points, security monitoring tools, and the SIEM appliance, working with the *Security Automation Domains* (See Figure 2). These would include, for example, the areas of malware detection, asset and event management. ConMon must first address these collective components to create a "First Generation" instantiation.

More specifically, a SIEM appliance provides the central core data processing capabilities to effectively coordinate all the inputs and outputs from across the IT enterprise. It manages the data integration and interpretation of all ConMon components. And, it provides the necessary visibility and intelligence for an active incident response capability.

End-point devices must be persistently visible to the applicable security devices. Together, these parts must align with the respective security controls described in NIST SP 800-53. The selected SIEM tool must accept these inputs and analyze them against defined security policy settings, recurring vulnerability scans, signature-based threats, and heuristic/activity-based analyses to ensure the environment's security posture. The SIEM outputs must support the IT environment's further visibility, conduct and disseminate vital intelligence, and alert leadership to any ongoing or imminent dangers. The expression above is designed to provide a conceptual representation of the cybersecurity professional attempting to ascertain effective ConMon implementation or develop a complete ConMon answer for an agency or corporation.

Additionally, the SIEM must distribute data feeds in near-real-time to analysts and critical leaders. It provides for multi-level "dashboard" data streams, and issues alert based upon prescribed policy settings. Once these base, First Generation functionalities are consistently aligning with the Security Automation Domains, then an organization or corporation can definitively express it meets the requirements of ConMon.

End-Points

It is necessary to identify hardware and software configuration items that must be known and constantly traceable before implementing ConMon within an enterprise IT environment. End-point visibility is not the hardware devices but the baseline software of each hardware device on the network.

Configuration Management is also a foundational requirement for any organization's security posture. Soundly implemented Configuration Management must be the basis of any complete CM implementation. At the beginning of any IS effort, cyber-professionals must know the enterprise's current "as-is" hardware and software component state. End-points must be protected and monitored because they are the most valuable target for would-be hackers and cyber thieves.

Configuration Management provides the baseline that establishes a means to identify potential compromise between the enterprise's end-points and the requisite security tools. "Organizations with a robust and effective [Configuration Management] process need to consider information security implications concerning the development and operation of information systems including hardware, software, applications, and documentation" (NIST-A, 2011).

The RMF requires the categorization of systems and data as high, moderate, or low regarding risk. The Federal Information Processing Standards (FIPS) Publication 199 methodology is typically used to establish data sensitivity levels in the federal government. FIPS 199 aids the cybersecurity professional in determining data protection standards of both end-points and the data stored in these respective parts. For example, a system that collects and retains sensitive data, such as financial information, requires a greater level of security. End-points must be recognized as repositories of highly valued data to cyber-threats.

Further, cyber-security professionals must be constantly aware of the "...administrative and technological costs of offering a high degree of protection for all federal systems..." (Ross, Katzke, & Toth, 2005). This is not a matter of recognizing the physical end-point alone but the value and associated costs of the virtual data stored, monitored, and protected continually. FIPS 199 assists system owners in determining whether a higher level of protection is warranted, with higher associated costs, based upon an overall FIPS 199 evaluation.

Security Tools

Security monitoring tools must identify in near-real-time an active threat. Examples include anti-virus or anti-malware applications used to monitor network and end-point activities. Products like McAfee and Symantec provide enterprise capabilities that help to identify and reduce threats.

Other security tools would address in whole or part the remaining NIST Security Automation Domains. These would include, for example, tools to provide asset visibility, vulnerability detection, patch management updates, etc. But it is also critical to recognize that even the best current security tools are not necessarily capable of defending against all attacks. New malware or zero-day attacks pose continual challenges to the cybersecurity workforce.

For example, DHS's EINSTEIN system would not have stopped the 2015 Office of Personnel Management breach. Even DHS's latest iteration of EINSTEIN, EINSTEIN 3, an advanced network monitoring and response system designed to protect federal governments' networks, would not have stopped that attack. "...EINSTEIN 3 would not have been able to catch a threat that [had] no known footprints, according to multiple industry experts" (Sternstein, 2015).

Until there is much greater integration and availability of cross-cutting intelligence and more capable security tools, can any single security tool ever be fully effective? The need for multiple security monitoring tools that provide "defense in depth" may be a better protective strategy. However, with various tools monitoring the same Security Automation Domains, such an approach will undoubtedly increase the costs of maintaining a secure agency or corporate IT environment. A determination of Return on Investment (ROI) balanced against a well-defined threat risk scoring approach is further needed at all levels of the federal and corporate IT workspace.

Security Controls

"Organizations are required to adequately mitigate the risk arising from the use of information and information systems in the execution of missions and business functions" (NIST, 2013). This is accomplished by selecting and implementing NIST SP 800-53, Revision 4, described security controls. (See Figure 4 below). They are organized into eighteen families to address sub-set security areas such as access control, physical security, incident response, etc. These controls are typically tailored to the security categorization by the respective system owner relying upon FIPS 199 categorization standards. A higher security categorization requires the more effective implementation of these controls.

ID	FAMILY	ID	FAMILY
AC	Access Control	MP	Media Protection
AT	Awareness and Training	PE	Physical and Environmental Protection
AU	Audit and Accountability	PL	Planning
CA	Security Assessment and Authorization	PS	Personnel Security
CM	Configuration Management	RA	Risk Assessment
CP	Contingency Planning	SA	System and Services Acquisition
IA	Identification and Authentication	SC	System and Communications Protection
IR	Incident Response	SI	System and Information Integrity
MA	Maintenance	PM	Program Management

* Note that these are all the control families required within DOD. Under the NIST 800-171 effort, not all control families are used or required.

Figure 4. Security Control Identifiers and Family Names, (NIST, 2013)

Security Information and Event Management (SIEM) Solutions

The SIEM tool plays a pivotal role in any viable "First Generation" implementation. Based on NIST and DHS guidance, a practical SIEM appliance must provide the following functionalities:

- "Aggregate data from "across a diverse set" of security tool sources;
- Analyze the multi-source data;
- Engage in explorations of data based on changing needs
- Make quantitative use of data for security (not just reporting) purposes, including the development and use of risk scores; and
- Maintain actionable awareness of the changing security situation on a real-time basis" (Levinson, 2011).

"Effectiveness is further enhanced when the output is formatted to provide information that is specific, measurable, actionable, relevant, and timely" (NIST, 2011). The SIEM device is the vital core of a complete solution that collects, analyzes, and alerts the cyber-professional of potential and actual dangers in their environment.

Several major SIEM solutions can effectively meet the requirements of NIST SP 800-137. They include products, for example, IBM® Security, Splunk®, and Hewlett Packard's® ArcSight® products.

SIEM products will continue to play a critical and evolving role in the demands for "...increased security and rapid response to events throughout the network" (McAfee® Foundstone Professional Services®, 2013). For example, Logrhythm ® was highly rated in the 2014 SIEM evaluation. Logrhythm® provided network event monitoring and alerts of potential security compromises. Implementing an enterprise-grade SIEM solution is necessary to meet growing cybersecurity requirements for auditing security logs and capabilities to respond to cyber-incidents. Improvements and upgrades of SIEM tools are critical to providing a more highly responsive ability for future generations of these appliances in the marketplace.

Next Generations

Future generations of ConMon would include specific expanded capabilities and functionalities of the SIEM device. These second generation and beyond evolutions would be more effective solutions in future dynamic and hostile network environments. Such advancements might also include increased access to a greater pool of threat database signature repositories or more expansive heuristics to identify active anomalies within a target network.

Another futuristic capability might include the use of Artificial Intelligence (AI). Improved capacities of a SIEM appliance with AI augmentation would further enhance human threat analysis and provide for more automated responsiveness. "The concept of predictive analysis involves using statistical methods and decision tools that analyze current and historical data to make predictions about future events..." (SANS Institute). The next generation would boost human response times and abilities to defend against attacks in a matter of milli-seconds vice hours.

Finally, in describing the next generations of ConMon, it is not only imperative to expand data, informational, and intelligence inputs for new and more capable SIEM products, but that input and corresponding data sets must also be thoroughly vetted for completeness and accuracy. Increased access to signature and heuristic activity-based analysis databases would provide more significant risk reduction. Greater support from private industry and the Intelligence Community would also be significant improvements for Agencies that are constantly struggling against a more capable and better-resourced threat.

ConMon will not be a reality until vendors and agencies integrate the right people, processes, and technologies. "Security needs to be positioned as an enabler of the organization—it must take its place alongside human resources, financial resources, sound business processes and strategies, information technology, and intellectual capital as the elements of success for accomplishing the mission" (Caralli, 2004). ConMon is not just a technical solution. It requires capable organizations with trained personnel, creating effective policies and procedures with the requisite technologies to stay ahead of the growing threats in cyberspace.

Figure 6 below provides a graphic depiction of ConMon components needed to create a holistic NIST SP 800-137-compliant solution; this demonstrates the First-Generation representation. Numerous vendors are describing that they have the "holy grail" solution. Still, until they can prove they meet this description in total, it is unlikely they have successfully implemented a comprehensive ConMon solution yet.

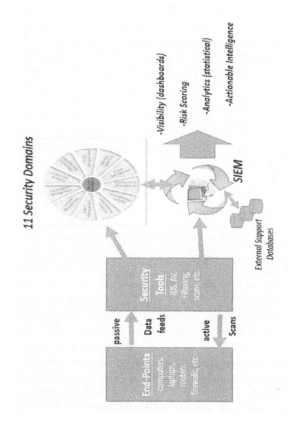

Figure 6. First Generation Continuous Monitoring

Endnotes for "Continuous Monitoring: A More Detailed Discussion"

Balakrishnan, B. (2015, October 6). *Insider Threat Mitigation Guidance*. Retrieved from SANS Institute Infosec Reading Room: https://www.sans.org/reading-room/whitepapers/monitoring/insider-threat-mitigation-guidance-36307

Caralli, R. A. (2004, December). *Managing Enterprise Security (CMU/SEI-2004-TN-046)*. Retrieved from Software Engineering Institute: http://www.sei.cmu.edu/reports/04tn046.pdf

Committee on National Security Systems. (2010, April 26). *National Information Assurance (IA) Glossary*. Retrieved from National Counterintelligence & Security Center: http://www.ncsc.gov/nittf/docs/CNSSI-4009_National_Information_Assurance.pdf

Department of Defense. (2014, March 12). *DOD Instructions 8510.01: Risk Management Framework (RMF) for DoD Information Technology (IT)*. Retrieved from Defense Technical Information Center (DTIC): http://www.dtic.mil/whs/directives/corres/pdf/851001_2014.pdf

GSA. (2012, January 27). *Continuous Monitoring Strategy & Guide, v1.1*. Retrieved from General Services Administration: http://www.gsa.gov/graphics/staffoffices/Continuous_Monitoring_Strategy_Guide_072712.pdf

Joint Medical Logistics Functional Development Center. (2015). JMLFDC Continuous Monitoring Strategy Plan and Procedure. Ft Detrick, MD.

Kavanagh, K. M., Nicolett, M., & Rochford, O. (2014, June 25). *Magic Quadrant for Security Information and Event Management*. Retrieved from Gartner: http://www.gartner.com/technology/reprints.do?id=1-1W8AO4W&ct=140627&st=sb&mkt_tok=3RkMMJWWfF9wsRolsqrJcO%2FhmjTEU5z17u8IWa%2B0gYkz2EFye%2BLIHETpodcMTcVkNb%2FYDBceEJhqyQJxPr3FKdANz8JpRhnqAA%3D%3D

Kolenko, M. M. (2016, February 18). *SPECIAL-The Human Element of Cybersecurity*. Retrieved from Homeland Security Today.US: http://www.hstoday.us/briefings/industry-news/single-article/special-the-human-element-of-cybersecurity/54008efd46e93863f54db0f7352dde2c.html

Levinson, B. (2011, October). *Federal Cybersecurity Best Practices Study: Information Security Continuous Monitoring*. Retrieved from Center for Regulatory Effectiveness: http://www.thecre.com/fisma/wp-content/uploads/2011/10/Federal-Cybersecurity-Best-Practice.ISCM_2.pdf

McAfee® Foundstone® Professional Services. (2013). *McAfee.* Retrieved from White Paper: Creating and Maintaining a SOC: http://www.mcafee.com/us/resources/white-papers/foundstone/wp-creating-maintaining-soc.pdf

NIST. (2011-A, August). *NIST SP 800-128: Guide for Security-Focused Configuration Management of Information Systems.* Retrieved from NIST Computer Security Resource Center: http://csrc.nist.gov/publications/nistpubs/800-128/sp800-128.pdf

NIST. (2011-B, September). *Special Publication 800-137: Information Security Continuous Monitoring (ISCM) for Federal Information Systems and Organizations.* Retrieved from NIST Computer Security Resource Center: http://csrc.nist.gov/publications/nistpubs/800-137/SP800-137-Final.pdf

NIST. (2012, January). *NIST Interagency Report 7756: CAESARS Framework Extension: An Enterprise Continuous Monitoring Technical Reference Model (Second Draft).* Retrieved from NIST Computer Resource Security Center: http://csrc.nist.gov/publications/drafts/nistir-7756/Draft-NISTIR-7756_second-public-draft.pdf

NIST. (2013, April). *NIST SP 800-53, Rev 4: Security and Privacy Controls for Federal Information Systems.* Retrieved from NIST: http://nvlpubs.nist.gov/nistpubs/SpecialPublications/NIST.SP.800-53r4.pdf

Ross, R., Katzke, S., & Toth, P. (2005, October 17). *The New FISMA Standards and Guidelines Changing the Dynamic of Information Security for the Federal Government.* Retrieved from Information Technology Promotion Agency of Japan: https://www.ipa.go.jp/files/000015362.pdf

Sann, W. (2016, January 8). *The Key Missing Piece of Your Cyber Strategy? Visibility.* Retrieved from Nextgov: http://www.nextgov.com/technology-news/tech-insider/2016/01/key-missing-element-your-cyber-strategy-visibility/124974/

SANS Institute. (2016, March 6). *Beyond Continuous Monitoring: Threat Modeling for Real-time Response.* Retrieved from SANS Institute: http://www.sans.org/reading-room/whitepapers/analyst/continuous-monitoring-threat-modeling-real-time-response-35185

Sternstein, A. (2015, January 6). *OPM Hackers Skirted Cutting-Edge Intrusion Detection System, Official Says.* Retrieved from Nextgov: http://www.nextgov.com/cybersecurity/2015/06/opm-hackers-skirted-cutting-edge-interior-intrusion-detection-official-says/114649/

Appendix C—Plan of Action & Milestones (POAM)

This appendix is an abbreviated description of what and how to create a good POAM response. It is designed to provide a structure for anyone developing a POAM for a company or agency. It describes how to approach the POAM development process and quickly formulate and track POAMs during their lifecycle. We suggest using the US Intelligence Community's *Intelligence Cycle* as a guide to handle POAM's from "cradle-to-grave." The process has been slightly modified to provide a more pertinent description for POAM creation. Still, this model is effective for the novice through professional cybersecurity or IT specialists who regularly work in this area.

This includes the following six stages:

1. **IDENTIFY:** Those controls that time, technology, or cost cannot be met to satisfy the unimplemented control.

2. **RESEARCH:** You now have decided the control will not meet your immediate NIST 800-171 needs. The typical initial milestone is to research what it is, how the federal government wants it implemented, and the need to identify the internal challenges the company may face from a people, process, or technology perspective.

3. **RECOMMEND:** At this phase, all research and analysis have been done and presumably well-documented. Typically, the cybersecurity team or business IT team will formulate recommended solutions to the System Owner, i.e., the business decision-makers such as the Chief Information or Operations Officer. The recommendations must be technically feasible, but cost and resources should be part of any recommendation.

4. **DECIDE:** At this point, company decision-makers not only approve of the approach to correct the security shortfall but have agreed to resource requirements to authorize the expenditures of funds and efforts.

5. **IMPLEMENT:** Finally, the solution is implemented, and the POAM is updated for closure. This should be reported to the Contract Office or its representative regularly.

6. **CONTINUAL IMPROVEMENT.** Like any process, it should be regularly reviewed and updated specifically to the needs and capabilities of the company or organization. This could include better templates, additional staffing, or more regular updates to management to ensure a thorough but supportive understanding of how cybersecurity meets the needs and mission of the business.

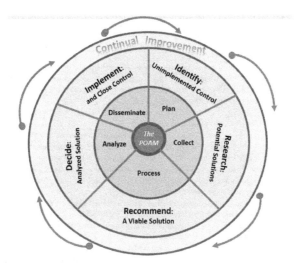

The POAM Lifecycle

We begin in the "Identify" section of the lifecycle process above. At this stage, several things may occur. Either the business owner or IT staff recognizes that the security control is not or cannot be immediately met. Alternatively, they employ an automated security tool, such as ACAS® or Nessus®, that identifies securities vulnerabilities within the IS. This could include finding that default passwords, like "password," have not been changed on an internal switch or router or that updated security patching has not occurred. Some automated systems will not only identify but recommend courses of action to mitigate or fix a security finding; always try to leverage those as soon as possible to secure your IT environment.

Mitigations must be based upon a strategy that is both specific and addresses the risk. The risk can be broad, such as widely known risks such as open-source intelligence threats from nation-state actors, or characteristic, based upon an automated tool, identifies weaknesses created by not applying a security patch for an Operating System or application. While the objective of developing a well-written POAM should be based upon a specific risk, this may not always be possible based upon the federal government's restriction for sharing "classified" information about the risk or threat. The mitigation should be commensurate with the threat or greater; more mitigating approaches, for example, the technical addition of better malware tools, more robust physical security controls of a site, or even better training of personnel, should always be a consideration in formulating an interim solution that reduces the threat but does not necessarily eliminate it.

Furthermore, **technical mitigations,** such as security hardware or software additions, should be about reducing the attack surface, impacts, or likelihoods of their exploit attempts. These should never be relied upon in total and should consider improvements in company or agency processes, procedures, and personnel practices.

Also, assumed in this stage is the act of documenting findings. The finding should be placed in a POAM template as the business moves through the lifecycle. For example, this could be done using documents created in Word®, but we recommend using a spreadsheet program that allows the easier filtering and management of the POAM. Spreadsheets afford greater flexibility during the "heavy lift" portion of formulating all POAM's not intended to be fixed immediately because of technical shortfalls (don't have the in-house technical expertise to setup Two Factor Authentication (2FA)) or because of financial limitations (the costs are currently prohibitive to implement the controls as required.)

The "research" phase includes technical analysis, Internet searches, market research, etc., regarding viable solutions to address the security control not being "compliant." This activity is typically part of the initial milestone established in the POAM. It may be added in the POAM and could be, for example: "Conduct an initial market research of candidate systems that can provide an affordable Two Factor Authentication (2FA) solution to meet security control 3.X.X." Another example might be: "The cybersecurity section will identify at least two candidate Data at Rest (DAR) solutions to protect the company's corporate and CUI data." These initial milestones are a normal part of any initial milestones that clearly describe reasonable actions to address non-complaint controls.

Another part of any milestone establishment action is to identify when this milestone is complete. Typically, milestones are done for 30 days, but if the complexity of such an activity requires additional time, ensure the company has identified reasonable periods of times with actual dates of *expected* completion; never use undefined milestones such as "next version update" or "The calendar Year 2020 in Quarter 4." Real dates are mandatory to manage findings supported by automated workflow or tracking applications truly.

At the "recommendation" phase, this is the time when the prior research has resulted in at least one solution, be it additional skilled personnel (people), enhanced company policies that manage the security control better (process), or a device that solves the control in part or total (technology). This should be part of this phase and the POAM template as a milestone with the expected completion date.

At the "decide" phase, company or agency decision-makers should approve a recommended solution. That decision should be documented in a configuration change tracking document, configuration management decision memorandum, or in the POAM itself. This should include approved resources, but most importantly, any funding decision should be acted upon as quickly as possible. While many of these suggestions may seem basic, documenting the decision so future personnel and management can understand the decision is often overlooked.

The "implementation" phase may become the most difficult. A lead should be designated to coordinate the specific activity to meet the control— it may not necessarily be a technical solution but a documentation development activity that creates a process to manage the POAM.

Implementation should also include basic programmatic considerations. This should consist of performance, schedule, cost, and risk:

- Performance: consider what success the solution is attempting to address. Can it send email alerts to users? Will the system shut down automatically once an intrusion is confirmed into the corporate network? Will the Incident Response Plan include notifications to law enforcement? Performance is always a significant and measurable means to ensure that the solution will address the POAM shortfall. Always try to measure performance specific to the actual control is being met.

- Schedule: Devise a plan based upon the developed milestones as reasonable and not unrealistic. As soon as a deviation becomes apparent, ensure that the POAM template is updated and approved by management, who has the authority to provide extensions to the current plan. This could include, for example, the Senior IT Manager, Chief Information Security Officer, or Chief Operating Officer.

- Cost: While it is assumed all funding has been provided early in the process, always ensure contingencies are in place to request additional funding. It is common in most IT programs to maintain a 15-20% funding reserve for emergencies. Otherwise, the Project Manager or lead will have to re-justify to management for additional funding late in the implementation portion of the cycle.

- Risk: This is not the risk identified, for example, by the review of security controls or automated scans of the system. This risk is specific to the program's success in accomplishing its goal to close the security finding. Risk should always focus on the performance, cost, and schedule risks as significant concerns. Consider creating a risk matrix or risk log to help during the implementation phase.

Finally, ensure that the company can satisfactorily implement its solution, close the control and notify the Contract Office of the completion. Typically, updates and notifications should occur at least once a quarter, but more often is appropriate for more highly impactful controls. Two-factor authentication and automated auditing, for example, are best updated as quickly as possible. This not only secures the company's network and IT environment but builds confidence with the government that security requirements are being met. A final area to consider in terms of best practices within cybersecurity, and more specifically in developing complete POAMs, is the area of continual improvement. Leveraging the legacy Intelligence Lifecycle process is an excellent example for IT and cybersecurity specialists to emulate. Everyone supporting this process should always be prepared to make changes or modifications that better represent the state and readiness of the system with its listing of POAMs.

Appendix D—Sample Risk Assessment (RA) Analysis Report

THRU: Ms. Smith, Information Systems Security Officer
FOR: Program Manager, Small-Widgets
FROM: Information Security Engineer, Bob New Hart, PE

Executive Summary

A Risk Analysis was completed on XX February XXXX for the Space Vehicle's Navigation and Communications subsystem. The static code review provided multiple artifacts to include the outputs from its preliminary and final reports. The final report identified near 100% correction (1 open warning) of any software coding weaknesses or vulnerabilities. Recommend approval.

Objective

- Recommend that Assessors [AUDITORS] conduct a review of provided artifacts and approve and accept this Risk Assessment (RA) following Risk Management Framework (RMF) specific to the RA-3 control.
- Request approval from Assessors [AUDITORS] about the current implementation and creation of a formalized RA process supporting the USSS 2020 program.

Analysis

The vendor and its subcontractor completed an *excellent* "static code" review and artifacts demonstration per RMF Control SA-11. The artifacts provided should become the basis and archetype for any future like RA efforts. The quality of the work completed specific to the Space Vehicle's Navigation, and Communications subsystem should be used to develop a more-defined RA process. The intent is to increase the security posture of the USSS 2020 in total and continue to help guide vendors to meet policy and contractual requirements.

1. RA Background Information:

    a. Risk Assessments are required throughout the system's life and are supposed to be updated as risks, and threats change against the specific system. These risks include version or build changes that occur during the normal process of maintaining and enhancing the readiness of the system to meet customer requirements.

b. System changes are required to be reflected in an updated RA IAW RMF control: RA-3. This includes "… modifications to the information system or environment of operation (including the identification of new threats and vulnerabilities) or other conditions that may impact the security state of the system.

c. A current process development effort is currently underway with the USSS 2020 and its subsystems. The effort requires some level of certainty of secure software development through formal artifacts provided by the developer.

d. The following documents are considered candidates that address security in whole or part by the developer:

    i. Changes impacting TRUSTED SOFTWARE DEVELOPMENT PROCESS (TSDP) hardware/components. This should include some form of attestation (signed) artifact by senior software development/quality assurance leadership that such development is in conformance with the Government approved secure process.

    ii. Completed Security Technical Implementation Guide (STIG) checklists for the APPLICATION SECURITY DEVELOPMENT STIG for all software. It should be signed and approved by the vendor's senior software development/quality assurance leadership.

    iii. Static code review of source code by government/industry-recognized tool. This should include, at a minimum, the final outputs from the tool to have an executive summary of findings and raw data subject to data rights limitations.

e. Space Vehicle's Navigation and Communications subsystem Software Risk Analysis:

    i. The artifact/file, Code-Analysis-Pre-Findings-rpt.pdf (See Attachment 1 for a listing of all artifacts), dated XX March 20XX, identified that the commercial static code analysis tool, CodeSonar2 (See Attachment 2), was used. The 8-software code sub-modules identified 397 active warnings across 220 total files per submodule. Of concern for cybersecurity purposes are the buffer overruns and integer overflows; the findings and numbers were constant across all submodules.

    ii. CodeSonar2 Analysis Report dated XX June 20XX, Code-Analysis-Final-rpt.pdf, identifies 0 active warnings after assuming coding updates were satisfactory. In this report, the outputs were parsed based on files versus submodule but identified the file count of 220 in Table 1, Summary for Recent Analyses. There were 220 total files scanned.

iii. In the Final Certification Report, <u>Final-Review-report.pdf</u>, XX November XXXX, all false positives were addressed, and only one final warning regarding "uninitialized variables" was identified in the file: oef_cobol213_string.cxx. While uninitialized variables pose a security risk, associated mitigating protections would protect the overall USSS 2020 from most outside cyber-attacks.

iv. Additionally, a Penetration Test was accomplished against the sub-system. While not required at the sub-system level, it demonstrates additional due diligence on the developer's part. The results of that effort appear acceptable.

v. Overall, it is reasonable to assume that all code functionality repairs, including high-interest security coding corrections, have been satisfactorily accomplished. Any risk to the <u>Space Vehicle's Navigation and Communications subsystem is suggested to be low.</u>

Conclusion

Request approval of a favorable RA for the <u>Space Vehicle's Navigation and Communications subsystem</u> of the USSS 2020 System.

Appendix E--Ten Success Recommendations

1. **Implement all Controls as best as possible.** They were devised to address the technical aspects of the control and, for example, its public reputation. While this is a voluntary regimen to industry, it provides an excellent model to secure a company or agency's IT environment. Also, be aware that a POAM is entirely acceptable if the solution cannot be implemented technologically or financially; let the POAM be "your friend."

2. **"Agility" occurs through "Continuous Monitoring" (ConMon) of the IT Environment.** While no company can monitor every aspect of a threat, either external or internal, it must embrace a continuous monitoring effort. This does not have to be a purely automated review of the technical controls, but manual checklists, reviews, and testing afford reasonable measures to protect IT assets and data.

3. **Understand the Principle of "Adequate Security."** The frameworks are looking for a "good faith' effort that the protections are in place. company will be conducting its own **"self-assessment"** and providing the contract office with the correct documents and artifacts that demonstrate "adequately" meeting the controls. *Have you done everything you can do (currently) to ensure the security posture is sufficient to prevent unauthorized access to the IT network?*

4. **Seek Greater than "Adequate."** While this book recommends minimum compliance, greater implementation of controls should be the objective. Always strive for a "fully compliant" solution using other mitigating controls through a "Defense in Depth" focus.

   > When implementing a secure IT environment, the System Owner (SO) should utilize the "Defense in Depth" principle to protect corporate or agency-sensitive data.

   > One of the least expensive security system solutions is a "Bastion Host." The Committee on National Security Systems (CNSS) Instruction No. 400920 defines a Bastion Host as "a special purpose computer on a network specifically designed and configured to withstand attacks." The computer generally hosts a single application, for example, a proxy server, and all other services are removed or limited to reduce the threat to the computer.

   > The second and broader protections in any IT environment is devised around the Defense in Depth (DID) principle, also called "layered defense," may include such additional protections to a company or agency's IT assets:
   >   - Physical protection (e.g., security fencing, alarms, badging systems, biometric controls, guards)

- Perimeter (e.g., firewalls, Intrusion Detection Systems (IDS), Intrusion Prevention Systems[13] (IPS), "Trusted Internet Connections")
- Data (e.g., Data Loss Prevention (DLP) programs, access controls, auditing)
- Application/Executables (e.g., **whitelisting** of authorized software, **blacklisting** blocking specified programs).

These solutions alone are not guaranteed to protect a network from outside threats fully and certainly won't prevent an insider threat with full rights and access. While they afford additional means to slow hackers and nation-state intruders, they are not total solutions. The government, and much of the cybersecurity community, strongly support the principle of **Defense in Depth (DID)**.

---

[13] Most IPS include IDS capabilities; the objective is if employed, an IPS will both "detect" and "prevent" the intrusion.

The Principle of Defense in Depth

DID relies upon multiple layers of technical and administrative controls and is designed to thwart a company or agency's network threats. Flaws inadvertently created by software developers create endless opportunities for hackers exploiting modern IT architectures. DID is intended to be a holistic solution to mitigate better and reduce risks.

5. **Be Honest.** This process is only as good as the effort put into it. To succeed, rely on subject matter experts, resource appropriately, and demand excellence in control implementation. Short cuts will only result in future weaknesses that make the company susceptible to cyber-attacks.

6. **Mitigate, Mitigate, Mitigate.** Don't rely only on a singular technical solution to meet the control in total. The weakest link in any organization is its people. Look to the People, Process, and Technology (PPT) triad as a holistic approach to a sound defense.

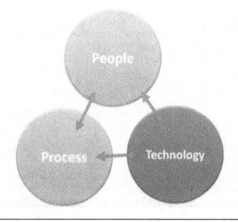

The PPT Model is the recommended guidance for answering many of the controls. While all solutions will not necessarily require a technological answer, consideration of the people (e.g., who? what skill sets? etc.) and process (e.g., notifications to senior management, action workflows, etc.) will meet many response requirements. The best responses will typically include the types and kinds of people assigned to oversee the control, the process or procedures that identify the workflow that will ensure that the control is met, and in some cases, the technology that will answer the control in part or whole.

7. **The Success of Cybersecurity Rests with the Leadership.** The failure of cybersecurity has been due to the lack of senior leadership involvement in the process. This should be their role in providing direction, seeking current threat updates, and especially resourcing to include trained personnel and dollars for the tools needed to protect the corporate infrastructure.

8. **It's Risk Management and not Risk Elimination.** It recognizes the risk (or threat) that is documented and captured as part of a POAM database that ensures awareness and appropriate responses within the company's IT environment and by its leadership—avoiding the identification, especially of incomplete control implementation, that creates the greatest risk.

9. **The Power of the POAM.** The POAM is not a "sign of weakness." It acknowledges where problems may arise and helps plan, resource, and focus on future resolution. (See Appendix C regarding POAM development).

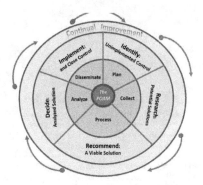

The POAM Lifecycle

10. **When working with the government, keeping it consistent and straightforward works.** Simplicity is your greatest ally when working with these new processes. Align responses to the controls as described.

Appendix F — Special Information Technology Systems (SPITS) Baseline Controls

These are the current major baseline controls to implement and secure SPITS-defined IT systems. The potential additions may occur at the discretion of the System Owner (SO) and the Authorizing Official (AO), who may identify enhancement to this control selection.

1. **RA-3: Risk Assessment**

   a. <u>SPECIFIC ACTIONS (OUTPUT):</u> Produce a Risk Assessment (RA) and analysis report (RAR) based on scans and other vulnerability detection activities as described in the control below.
   b. Conduct an assessment of risk, including the likelihood and magnitude of harm from the unauthorized access, use, disclosure, disruption, modification, or destruction of the information system and the information it processes, stores, or transmits.
   c. Review risk assessment results <u>annually</u>; and,
   d. Update the risk assessment <u>annually</u> or whenever there are significant changes to the information system or environment of operation (including identifying new threats and vulnerabilities), or other conditions that may impact the system's security state.

2. **RA-5: Vulnerability Scanning**

   a. <u>SPECIFIC ACTIONS (OUTPUT):</u> The developer will demonstrate it has completed the DOD Application Security Development (ASD) STIG checklist; it will be signed/approved by the designated developer Software Quality Assurance Engineer or like representative. Additionally, the developer will use secure code scanning software (e.g., HP Fortify®) and provide the executive and raw scans to meet this control.
   b. Scan for vulnerabilities in the information system and **hosted application** [specific to SPM] are reviewed every three years or when a modification is executed. [Requires a new Risk Assessment [RA-2]] and when new vulnerabilities potentially affecting the system/applications are identified and reported;
   c. Employ vulnerability scanning tools and techniques that facilitate interoperability among tools and automate parts of the vulnerability management process by using standards for Software flaws and improper configurations; formatting checklists and test procedures; and measuring vulnerability impact; analyze vulnerability scan reports and results from security control assessments;
   d. Remediate vulnerabilities within <u>60 days</u> (RECOMMENDED) following an organizational assessment of risk; and
   e. Share information obtained from the vulnerability scanning process and security control assessments.

3. **CM-6: Document Configuration Settings**

   a. <u>SPECIFIC ACTIONS (OUTPUT):</u> Establish and document configuration settings for information technology products [SPITS solution] employed within the information system using a <u>security configuration checklist </u>(**developer produced in addition to ASD requirements**) that reflects the most restrictive mode consistent with operational requirements;
   b. Implement configuration settings;
   c. Identify, document, and approve any deviations from established configuration settings for SPITS Modules based on operational requirements; and
   d. Monitor and control changes

4. **SA-11: Security Testing and Evaluation**

   a. <u>SPECIFIC ACTIONS (OUTPUT):</u> The developer will provide test plans and a report demonstrating it has conducted code level review and analysis and has mitigated findings. There should be no critical code vulnerabilities (e.g., buffer overflow, SQL injection, etc.). All other results will be mitigated with an accepted POAM.
   b. Create and implement a security assessment plan;
   c. Perform unit and integration code analysis, review, testing, and development of embedded software and all associated hardware and firmware modules to ensure secure code delivery;
   d. Produce evidence of the execution of the Security Assessment Plan (SAP) and the security testing/evaluation results.
   e. Implement a verifiable flaw remediation process; and
   f. Correct flaws identified during security testing/evaluation.

5. **SA-12 Supply Chain Protection**

   a. <u>SPECIFIC ACTIONS(OUTPUT):</u> The organization protects against supply chain threats to the information system, system component, or information system service by employing security safeguards as part of a comprehensive, defense-in-breadth information security strategy. This should include a "Supply Chain Risk Management" procedural document that identifies internal (quality assurance reviews) and external (logistics reviews of all purchases) that ensures all IT components meet DOD/DISA approved products lists for both hardware and software. It shall identify all current efforts and challenges facing the organization and suggested best practices to ensure only approved products are obtained for the designated system.
   b. Information systems (including system components that compose those systems) must be protected throughout the system development life cycle (i.e., during

design, development, manufacturing, packaging, assembly, distribution, system integration, operations, maintenance, and retirement). The protection of organizational information systems is accomplished through threat awareness by identifying, managing, and reducing vulnerabilities at each phase of the life cycle and using complementary, mutually reinforcing strategies to respond to risk.

c. Organizations consider implementing a standardized process to address supply chain risk concerning information systems and system components and educate the acquisition workforce on threats, risks, and required security controls. Organizations use the acquisition/procurement processes to require supply chain entities to implement necessary security safeguards to (i) reduce the likelihood of unauthorized modifications at each stage in the supply chain; (ii) protect information systems and information system components before taking delivery of such systems/components.

d. This control also applies to information system services. Security safeguards include, for example, (i) security controls for development systems, development facilities, and external connections to development systems; (ii) vetting development personnel; and (iii) use of tamper-evident packaging during shipping/warehousing. Methods for reviewing and protecting development plans, evidence, and documentation are commensurate with the information system's security category or classification level. Contracts may specify documentation protection requirements.

6. SI-2: Flaw Remediation

a. <u>SPECIFIC ACTIONS:</u> The developer must demonstrate that it has corrected all flaws and there is a policy/procedure developed as part of the overall system configuration management plan/process.

b. Identify, report, and correct information system flaws;

c. Test software and firmware updates related to flaw remediation for effectiveness and potential side effects before installation;

d. Install security-relevant software and firmware updates within <u>60 days</u> (RECOMMENDED) of the release of the updates; and

e. Incorporate flaw remediation into the organizational configuration management process.

7. SI-16 Memory Protection

a. <u>SPECIFIC ACTIONS(OUTPUT):</u> The developer implements a candidate security safeguard, hardware, or software enforced solution. It will be approved/signed by the developer's senior software developer or duly assigned representative and approved by the System Owner/Program Manager. This will ensure the approved solution protects system memory from unauthorized code execution.

b. (Some adversaries launch attacks with the intent of executing code in non-executable regions of memory or in memory locations that are prohibited. Security safeguards employed to protect memory include, for example, data execution prevention and address space layout randomization.) Data execution prevention safeguards can either be hardware-enforced or software-enforced, with hardware providing the greater strength of mechanism.

8. SI-11 Error Handling

a. SPECIFIC ACTIONS: Demonstrate generation of error messages that provide information necessary for corrective actions without revealing information that adversaries could exploit and shows error messages only to assigned System Administrator (SA), ISSM, and/or ISSO to ensure the developer addresses error identification before operational deployment.
b. Organizations carefully consider the structure/content of error messages. The extent to which information systems can identify and handle error conditions is guided by organizational policy and operational requirements. Information that adversaries could exploit includes, for example, erroneous logon attempts with passwords entered by mistake as the username, mission/business information that can be derived from (if not stated explicitly by) information recorded, and personal information such as account numbers, social security numbers, and credit card numbers. In addition, error messages may provide a covert channel for transmitting the information.

9. SC-8 Transmission Confidentiality and Integrity

a. SPECIFIC ACTIONS: The information system protects the confidentiality and integrity of transmitted information. This will be demonstrated by some form of DOD/NSA encryption standard mandated to preserve the data type identified.
b. This control applies to internal and external networks and all types of information system modules from which information can be transmitted (e.g., servers, mobile devices, notebook computers, printers, copiers, scanners, facsimile machines). Communication paths outside the physical protection of a controlled boundary are exposed to the possibility of interception and modification. Protecting organizational information's confidentiality and/or integrity can be accomplished by physical means (e.g., employing protected distribution systems) or logical means (e.g., using encryption techniques).
c. Organizations relying on commercial providers offering transmission services as commodity services rather than fully dedicated services (i.e., services that can be highly specialized to individual customer needs) may find it challenging to obtain the necessary assurances regarding the implementation of needed security controls for transmission confidentiality/integrity. In such situations, organizations determine what confidentiality/integrity services are available in standard, commercial

telecommunication service packages. Suppose it is infeasible or impractical to obtain the necessary security controls and assurances of control effectiveness through appropriate contracting vehicles. In that case, organizations implement appropriate compensating security controls or explicitly accept the additional risk.

Appendix G– NIST 800-171 Compliance Checklist

The following compliance checklist is intended to provide a guide to conduct a "self-assessment" of the company's overall cybersecurity posture as required by NIST 800-171.

*Assessment Method: Refer to NIST 800-171A, *Assessing Security Requirements for Controlled Unclassified Information*, which describes types and means to self-validate the control. The three assessment methods are: examine, interview and test.

Control #	Description	Assessment Method*	Document (e.g., SSP or Co. Procedure Guide)	Page #	Reviewed By	Validated By
Access Control (AC)						
3.1.1	Limit information system access to authorized users, processes acting on behalf of authorized users, or devices (including other information systems)					
3.1.1[a]	Authorized users are identified.					
3.1.1[b]	Processes acting on behalf of authorized users are identified.					
3.1.1[c]	Devices (and other systems) authorized to connect to the system are identified.					
3.1.1[d]	System access is limited to authorized users.					
3.1.1[e]	System access is limited to processes acting					

	on behalf of authorized users.	
3.1.1[f]	System access is limited to authorized devices (including other systems).	
3.1.1[a]	Authorized users are identified.	
3.1.2	**Limit information system access to the types of transactions and functions that authorized users are permitted to execute**	
3.1.2[a]	The types of transactions and functions that authorized users are permitted to execute are defined.	
3.1.2[b]	System access is limited to the defined types of transactions and functions for authorized users.	
3.1.3	**Control the flow of CUI in accordance with approved authorizations**	
3.1.3[a]	Information flow control policies are defined.	
3.1.3[b]	Methods and enforcement mechanisms for controlling the flow of CUI are defined.	
3.1.3[c]	Designated sources and	

	destinations (e.g., networks, individuals, and devices) for CUI within the system and between interconnected systems are identified.	
3.1.3[d]	Authorizations for controlling the flow of CUI are defined.	
3.1.3[e]	Approved authorizations for controlling the flow of CUI are enforced.	
3.1.4	**Separate the duties of individuals to reduce the risk of malevolent activity without collusion**	
3.1.4[a]	The duties of individuals requiring separation are defined.	
3.1.4[b]	Responsibilities for duties that require separation are assigned to separate individuals.	
3.1.4[c]	Access privileges that enable individuals to exercise the duties that require separation are granted to separate individuals.	
3.1.5	*Employ the principle of least privilege, including for*	

	specific security functions and privileged accounts	
3.1.5[a]	Privileged accounts are identified.	
3.1.5[b]	Access to privileged accounts is authorized in accordance with the principle of least privilege.	
3.1.5[c]	Security functions are identified.	
3.1.5[d]	Access to security functions is authorized in accordance with the principle of least privilege.	
3.1.6	*Use non-privileged accounts or roles when accessing nonsecurity functions*	
3.1.6[a]	Nonsecurity functions are identified.	
3.1.6[b]	Users are required to use non-privileged accounts or roles when accessing nonsecurity functions.	
3.1.7	**Prevent non-privileged users from executing privileged functions and audit the execution of such functions**	

3.1.7[a]	Privileged functions are defined.		
3.1.7[b]	Non-privileged users are defined.		
3.1.7[c]	Non-privileged users are prevented from executing privileged functions.		
3.1.7[d]	The execution of privileged functions is captured in audit logs.		
3.1.8	**Limit unsuccessful logon attempts**		
3.1.8[a]	The means of limiting unsuccessful logon attempts is defined.		
3.1.8[b]	The defined means of limiting unsuccessful logon attempts is implemented.		
3.1.9	**Provide privacy and security notices consistent with applicable CUI rules**		
3.1.9[a]	Privacy and security notices required by CUI-specified rules are identified, consistent, and associated with the specific CUI category.		
3.1.9[b]	Privacy and security notices are displayed.		
3.1.10	**Use session lock with**		

	pattern-hiding displays to prevent access/viewing of data after period of inactivity	
3.1.10[a]	The period of inactivity after which the system initiates a session lock is defined.	
3.1.10[b]	Access to the system and viewing of data is prevented by initiating a session lock after the defined period of inactivity.	
3.1.10[c]	Previously visible information is concealed via a pattern-hiding display after the defined period of inactivity.	
3.1.11	**Terminate (automatically) a user session after a defined condition**	
3.1.11[a]	Conditions requiring a user session to terminate are defined.	

3.1.11[b]	A user session is automatically terminated after any of the defined conditions occur.	

Control #	Description	Assessment Method*	Document (e.g., SSP or Co. Procedure Guide)	Page #	Reviewed By	Validated By
Access Control (AC)						
3.1.12	**Monitor and control remote access sessions**					
3.1.12[a]	Remote access sessions are permitted.					
3.1.12[b]	The types of permitted remote access are identified.					
3.1.12[c]	Remote access sessions are controlled.					
3.1.12[d]	Remote access sessions are monitored.					
3.1.13	**Employ cryptographic mechanisms to protect the confidentiality of remote access sessions**					
3.1.13[a]	Cryptographic mechanisms to protect the confidentiality of remote access sessions are identified.					
3.1.13[b]	Cryptographic mechanisms to protect the confidentiality of remote access sessions are implemented.					
3.1.14	**Route remote access via managed access control points**					
3.1.14[a]	Managed access control points are identified and implemented.					
3.1.14[b]	Remote access is routed through managed network access control points.					
3.1.15	**Authorize remote execution of privileged commands and remote access to security-relevant information**					
3.1.15[a]	Privileged commands authorized for remote execution are identified.					
3.1.15[b]	Security-relevant information authorized to be accessed remotely is identified.					
3.1.15[c]	The execution of the identified privileged commands via remote access is authorized.					

3.1.15[d]	Access to the identified security-relevant information via remote access is authorized.	
3.1.16	**Authorize wireless access prior to allowing such connections**	
3.1.16[a]	Wireless access points are identified.	
3.1.16[b]	Wireless access is authorized prior to allowing such connections.	
3.1.17	**Protect wireless access using authentication and encryption**	
3.1.17[a]	Wireless access to the system is protected using authentication.	
3.1.17[b]	Wireless access to the system is protected using encryption.	
3.1.18	**Control connection of mobile devices**	
3.1.18[a]	Mobile devices that process, store, or transmit CUI are identified.	
3.1.18[b]	Mobile device connections are authorized.	
3.1.18[c]	Mobile device connections are monitored and logged.	
3.1.19	**Encrypt CUI on mobile devices**	
3.1.19[a]	Mobile devices and mobile computing platforms that process, store, or transmit CUI are identified.	
3.1.19[b]	Encryption is employed to protect CUI on identified mobile devices and mobile computing platforms.	
3.1.20[a]	Connections to external systems are identified.	
3.1.20[b]	The use of external systems is identified.	
3.1.20[c]	Connections to external systems are verified.	
3.1.20[d]	The use of external systems is verified.	
3.1.20[e]	Connections to external systems are controlled/limited.	
3.1.20[f]	The use of external systems is controlled/limited.	
3.1.20[a]	Connections to external systems are identified.	

3.1.21	Limit use of organizational portable storage devices on external systems	
3.1.21[a]	The use of portable storage devices containing CUI on external systems is identified and documented.	
3.1.21[b]	Limits on the use of portable storage devices containing CUI on external systems are defined.	
3.1.21[c]	The use of portable storage devices containing CUI on external systems is limited as defined.	
3.1.22	Control CUI posted or processed on publicly accessible systems	
3.1.22[a]	Individuals authorized to post or process information on publicly accessible systems are identified.	
3.1.22[b]	Procedures to ensure CUI is not posted or processed on publicly accessible systems are identified.	
3.1.22[c]	A review process is in place prior to posting of any content to publicly accessible systems.	
3.1.22[d]	Content on publicly accessible systems is reviewed to ensure that it does not include CUI.	
3.1.22[e]	Mechanisms are in place to remove and address improper posting of CUI.	
3.1.22[a]	Individuals authorized to post or process information on publicly accessible systems are identified.	

Control #	Description	Assessment Method*	Document (e.g., SSP or Co. Procedure Guide)	Page #	Reviewed By	Validated By
Awareness & Training (AT)						
3.2.1	**Ensure that managers, systems administrators, and users of organizational information systems are made aware of the security risks associated with their activities and of the applicable policies, standards, and procedures related to the security of organizational information systems**					
3.2.1[a]	Security risks associated with organizational activities involving CUI are identified.					
3.2.1[b]	Policies, standards, and procedures related to the security of the system are identified.					
3.2.1[c]	Managers, systems administrators, and users of the system are made aware of the security risks associated with their activities.					

3.2.1[d]	Managers, systems administrators, and users of the system are made aware of the applicable policies, standards, and procedures related to the security of the system.	
3.2.2	**Ensure that organizational personnel are adequately trained to carry out their assigned information security-related duties and responsibilities**	
3.2.2[a]	Information security-related duties, roles, and responsibilities are defined.	
3.2.2[b]	Information security-related duties, roles, and responsibilities are assigned to designated personnel.	
3.2.2[c]	Personnel are adequately trained to carry out their assigned information security-related duties, roles, and responsibilities.	
3.2.3	**Provide security awareness training on recognizing and reporting**	

	potential indicators of insider threat	
3.2.3[a]	Potential indicators associated with insider threats are identified.	
3.2.3[b]	Security awareness training on recognizing and reporting potential indicators of insider threat is provided to managers and employees.	

Control #	Description	Assessment Method*	Document (e.g. SSP or Co. Procedure Guide)	Page #	Reviewed By	Validated By
Audit & Accountability (AU)						
3.3.1	**Create, protect, and retain information system audit records to the extent needed to enable the monitoring, analysis, investigation, and reporting of unlawful, unauthorized, or inappropriate information system activity**					
3.3.1[a]	Audit logs needed (i.e., event types to be logged) to enable the monitoring, analysis, investigation, and reporting of unlawful or unauthorized system activity are specified.					
3.3.1[b]	The content of audit records needed to support monitoring, analysis, investigation, and reporting of unlawful or unauthorized system activity is defined.					
3.3.1[c]	Audit records are created (generated).					
3.3.1[d]	Audit records, once created, contain the defined content.					
3.3.1[e]	Retention requirements for audit records are defined.					
3.3.1[f]	Audit records are retained as defined.					
3.3.2	**Ensure that the actions of individual**					

	information system users can be uniquely traced to those users, so they can be held accountable for their actions	
3.3.2[a]	The content of the audit records needed to support the ability to uniquely trace users to their actions is defined.	
3.3.2[b]	Audit records, once created, contain the defined content.	
3.3.3	**Review and update audited events**	
3.3.3[a]	A process for determining when to review logged events is defined.	
3.3.3[b]	Event types being logged are reviewed in accordance with the defined review process.	
3.3.3[c]	Event types being logged are updated based on the review.	
3.3.4	**Alert in the event of an audit process failure**	
3.3.4[a]	Personnel or roles to be alerted in the event of an audit logging process failure are identified.	
3.3.4[b]	Types of audit logging process failures for which alert will be generated are defined.	
3.3.4[c]	Identified personnel or roles are alerted in the event of an audit logging process failure.	
3.3.5	**Correlate audit review, analysis, and reporting processes for investigation and**	

	response to indications of inappropriate, suspicious, or unusual activity	
3.3.5[a]	Audit record review, analysis, and reporting processes for investigation and response to indications of unlawful, unauthorized, suspicious, or unusual activity are defined.	
3.3.5[b]	Defined audit record review, analysis, and reporting processes are correlated.	
3.3.6	**Provide audit reduction and report generation to support on-demand analysis and reporting**	
3.3.6[a]	An audit record reduction capability that supports on-demand analysis is provided.	
3.3.6[b]	A report generation capability that supports on-demand reporting is provided.	
3.3.7	**Provide an information system capability that compares and synchronizes internal system clocks with an authoritative source to generate time stamps for audit records**	
3.3.7[a]	Internal system clocks are used to generate time stamps for audit records.	

3.3.7[b]	An authoritative source with which to compare and synchronize internal system clocks is specified.	
3.3.7[c]	Internal system clocks used to generate time stamps for audit records are compared to and synchronized with the specified authoritative time source.	
3.3.8	**Protect audit information and audit tools from unauthorized access, modification, and deletion**	
3.3.8[a]	Audit information is protected from unauthorized access.	
3.3.8[b]	Audit information is protected from unauthorized modification.	
3.3.8[c]	Audit information is protected from unauthorized deletion.	
3.3.8[d]	Audit logging tools are protected from unauthorized access.	
3.3.8[e]	Audit logging tools are protected from unauthorized modification.	
3.3.8[f]	Audit logging tools are protected from unauthorized deletion.	
3.3.9	**Limit management of audit functionality to a subset of privileged users**	
3.3.9[a]	A subset of privileged users granted access to manage audit logging functionality is defined.	

3.3.9[b]	Management of audit logging functionality is limited to the defined subset of privileged users.

Control #	Description	Assessment Method*	Document (e.g., SSP or Co. Procedure Guide)	Page #	Reviewed By	Validated By
Configuration Management (CM)						
3.4.1	**Establish and maintain baseline configurations and inventories of organizational information systems (including hardware, software, firmware, and documentation) throughout the respective system development life cycles**					
3.4.1[a]	A baseline configuration is established.					
3.4.1[b]	The baseline configuration includes hardware, software, firmware, and documentation.					
3.4.1[c]	The baseline configuration is maintained (reviewed and updated) throughout the system development life cycle.					
3.4.1[d]	A system inventory is established.					
3.4.1[e]	The system inventory includes hardware, software, firmware, and documentation.					
3.4.1[f]	The inventory is maintained (reviewed and updated) throughout the system development life cycle.					
3.4.2	**Establish and enforce security configuration settings for information technology products employed in organizational information systems**					

3.4.2[a]	Security configuration settings for information technology products employed in the system are established and included in the baseline configuration.	
3.4.2[b]	Security configuration settings for information technology products employed in the system are enforced.	
3.4.3	**Track, review, approve/disapprove, and audit changes to information systems**	
3.4.3[a]	Changes to the system are tracked.	
3.4.3[b]	Changes to the system are reviewed.	
3.4.3[c]	Changes to the system are approved or disapproved.	
3.4.3[d]	Changes to the system are logged.	
3.4.4	**Analyze the security impact of changes prior to implementation**	
3.4.5	**Define, document, approve, and enforce physical and logical access restrictions associated with changes to the information system**	
3.4.5[a]	Physical access restrictions associated with changes to the system are defined.	
3.4.5[b]	Physical access restrictions associated with changes to the system are documented.	
3.4.5[c]	Physical access restrictions associated with changes to the system are approved.	
3.4.5[d]	Physical access restrictions associated with changes to the system are enforced.	

3.4.5[e]	Logical access restrictions associated with changes to the system are defined.	
3.4.5[f]	Logical access restrictions associated with changes to the system are documented.	
3.4.5[g]	Logical access restrictions associated with changes to the system are approved.	
3.4.5[h]	Logical access restrictions associated with changes to the system are enforced.	
3.4.6	**Employ the principle of least functionality by configuring the information system to provide only essential capabilities**	
3.4.6[a]	Essential system capabilities are defined based on the principle of least functionality.	
3.4.6[b]	The system is configured to provide only the defined essential capabilities.	
3.4.7	**Restrict, disable, and prevent the use of nonessential programs, functions, ports, protocols, and services**	
3.4.7[a]	Essential programs are defined.	
3.4.7[b]	The use of nonessential programs is defined.	
3.4.7[c]	The use of nonessential programs is restricted, disabled, or prevented as defined.	
3.4.7[d]	Essential functions are defined.	
3.4.7[e]	The use of nonessential functions is defined.	
3.4.7[f]	The use of nonessential functions is restricted,	

	disabled, or prevented as defined.	
3.4.7[g]	Essential ports are defined.	
3.4.7[h]	The use of nonessential ports is defined.	
3.4.7[i]	The use of nonessential ports is restricted, disabled, or prevented as defined.	
3.4.7[j]	Essential protocols are defined.	
3.4.7[k]	The use of nonessential protocols is defined.	
3.4.7[l]	The use of nonessential protocols is restricted, disabled, or prevented as defined.	
3.4.7[m]	Essential services are defined.	
3.4.7[n]	The use of nonessential services is defined.	
3.4.7[o]	The use of nonessential services is restricted, disabled, or prevented as defined.	
3.4.8	**Apply deny-by-exception (blacklist) policy to prevent the use of unauthorized software or deny all, permit-by-exception (whitelisting) policy to allow the execution of authorized software**	
3.4.8[a]	A policy specifying whether whitelisting or blacklisting is to be implemented is specified.	
3.4.8[b]	The software allowed to execute under whitelisting or denied use under blacklisting is specified.	
3.4.8[c]	Whitelisting to allow the execution of authorized software or blacklisting to prevent the use of unauthorized software is implemented as specified.	

3.4.9	Control and monitor user-installed software
3.4.9[a]	A policy for controlling the installation of software by users is established.
3.4.9[b]	Installation of software by users is controlled based on the established policy.
3.4.9[c]	Installation of software by users is monitored.

Control #	Description	Assessment Method*	Document (e.g., SSP or Co. Procedure Guide)	Page #	Reviewed By	Validated By
Identification & Authentication (IA)						
3.5.1	**Identify information system users, processes acting on behalf of users, or devices**					
3.5.1[a]	System users are identified.					
3.5.1[b]	Processes acting on behalf of users are identified.					
3.5.1[c]	Devices accessing the system are identified.					
3.5.2	**Authenticate (or verify) the identities of those users, processes, or devices, as a prerequisite to allowing access to organizational information systems**					
3.5.2[a]	The identity of each user is authenticated or verified as a prerequisite to system access.					
3.5.2[b]	The identity of each process acting on behalf of a user is authenticated or verified as a prerequisite to system access.					
3.5.2[c]	The identity of each device accessing or connecting to the system is authenticated or verified as a prerequisite to system access.					
3.5.3	**Use multifactor authentication for local and network access to privileged accounts and for network access to**					

	non-privileged accounts	
3.5.3[a]	Privileged accounts are identified.	
3.5.3[b]	Multifactor authentication is implemented for local access to privileged accounts.	
3.5.3[c]	Multifactor authentication is implemented for network access to privileged accounts.	
3.5.3[d]	Multifactor authentication is implemented for network access to non-privileged accounts.	
3.5.4	**Employ replay-resistant authentication mechanisms for network access to privileged and nonprivileged accounts**	
3.5.5	**Prevent reuse of identifiers for a defined period**	
3.5.5[a]	A period within which identifiers cannot be reused is defined.	
3.5.5[b]	Reuse of identifiers is prevented within the defined period.	
3.5.6	**Disable identifiers after a defined period of inactivity**	
3.5.6[a]	A period of inactivity after which an identifier is disabled is defined.	
3.5.6[b]	Identifiers are disabled after the defined period of inactivity.	
3.5.7	**Enforce a minimum password**	

	complexity and change of characters when new passwords are created	
3.5.7[a]	Password complexity requirements are defined.	
3.5.7[b]	Password change of character requirements are defined.	
3.5.7[c]	Minimum password complexity requirements as defined are enforced when new passwords are created.	
3.5.7[d]	Minimum password change of character requirements as defined are enforced when new passwords are created.	
3.5.8	**Prohibit password reuse for a specified number of generations**	
3.5.8[a]	The number of generations during which a password cannot be reused is specified.	
3.5.8[b]	Reuse of passwords is prohibited during the specified number of generations.	
3.5.9	**Allow temporary password use for system logons with an immediate change to a permanent password**	
3.5.10	**Store and transmit only encrypted representation of passwords**	
3.5.10[a]	Passwords are cryptographically protected in storage.	

3.5.10[b]	Passwords are cryptographically protected in transit.	
3.5.11.	**Obscure feedback of authentication information**	

Control #	Description	Assessment Method*	Document (e.g., SSP or Co. Procedure Guide)	Page #	Reviewed By	Validated By
Incident Response (IR)						
3.6.1	**Establish an operational incident-handling capability for organizational information systems that includes adequate preparation, detection, analysis, containment, recovery, and user response activities**					
3.6.1[a]	An operational incident-handling capability is established.					
3.6.1[b]	The operational incident-handling capability includes preparation.					
3.6.1[c]	The operational incident-handling capability includes detection.					
3.6.1[d]	The operational incident-handling capability includes analysis.					
3.6.1[e]	The operational incident-handling capability includes containment.					
3.6.1[f]	The operational incident-handling capability includes recovery.					
3.6.1[g]	The operational incident-handling capability includes user response activities.					
3.6.2	**Track, document, and report incidents to appropriate officials and/or authorities both internal and external to the organization**					
3.6.2[a]	Incidents are tracked.					
3.6.2[b]	Incidents are documented.					

3.6.2[c]	Authorities to whom incidents are to be reported are identified.	
3.6.2[d]	Organizational officials to whom incidents are to be reported are identified.	
3.6.2[e]	Identified authorities are notified of incidents.	
3.6.2[f]	Identified organizational officials are notified of incidents.	
3.6.3	**Test the organizational incident response capability**	

Control #	Description	Assessment Method*	Document (e.g., SSP or CO Procedure Guide)	Page #	Reviewed By	Validated By
Maintenance (MA)						
3.7.1	**Perform maintenance on organizational information systems**					
3.7.2	**Provide effective controls on the tools, techniques, mechanisms, and personnel used to conduct information system maintenance**					
3.7.2[a]	Tools used to conduct system maintenance are controlled.					
3.7.2[b]	Techniques used to conduct system maintenance are controlled.					
3.7.2[c]	Mechanisms used to conduct system maintenance are controlled.					
3.7.2[d]	Personnel used to conduct system maintenance are controlled.					
3.7.3	**Ensure equipment removed for off-site maintenance is sanitized of any CUI**					
3.7.4	**Check media containing diagnostic and test programs for malicious code before the media are used in the information system**					
3.7.5	**Require multifactor authentication to establish nonlocal maintenance sessions via external network connections and terminate such connections when**					

	nonlocal maintenance is complete
3.7.5[a]	Multifactor authentication is used to establish nonlocal maintenance sessions via external network connections.
3.7.5[b]	Nonlocal maintenance sessions established via external network connections are terminated when nonlocal maintenance is complete.
3.7.6	**Supervise the maintenance activities of maintenance personnel without required access authorization**

Control #	Description	Assessment Method*	Document (e.g., SSP or Co. Procedure Guide)	Page #	Reviewed By	Validated By

Media Protection (MP)

Control #	Description					
3.8.1	Protect (i.e., physically control and securely store) information system media containing CUI, both paper and digital					
3.8.1[a]	Paper media containing CUI is physically controlled.					
3.8.1[b]	Digital media containing CUI is physically controlled.					
3.8.1[c]	Paper media containing CUI is securely stored.					
3.8.1[d]	Digital media containing CUI is securely stored.					
3.8.2	Limit access to CUI on information system media to authorized users					
3.8.3	Sanitize or destroy information system media containing CUI before disposal or release for reuse					
3.8.3[a]	System media containing CUI is sanitized or destroyed before disposal.					
3.8.3[b]	System media containing CUI is sanitized before it is released for reuse.					
3.8.4	Mark media with necessary CUI markings and distribution limitations					
3.8.4[a]	Media containing CUI is marked with applicable CUI markings.					

3.8.4[b]	Media containing CUI is marked with distribution limitations.
3.8.5	**Control access to media containing CUI and maintain accountability for media during transport outside of controlled areas**
3.8.5[a]	Access to media containing CUI is controlled.
3.8.5[b]	Accountability for media containing CUI is maintained during transport outside of controlled areas.
3.8.6	**Implement cryptographic mechanisms to protect the confidentiality of CUI stored on digital media during transport unless otherwise protected by alternative physical safeguards**
3.8.7	**Control the use of removable media on information system components**
3.8.8	**Prohibit the use of portable storage devices when such devices have no identifiable owner**
3.8.9	**Protect the confidentiality of backup CUI at storage locations**

Control #	Description	Assessment Method*	Document (e.g. SSP or CUI Procedure Guide)	Page #	Review ed By	Validat ed By
Personnel Security (PS)						
3.9.1	**Screen individuals prior to authorizing access to information systems containing CUI**					
3.9.2	**Ensure that CUI and information systems containing CUI are protected during and after personnel actions such as terminations and transfers**					
3.9.2[a]	A policy and/or process for terminating system access and any credentials coincident with personnel actions is established.					
3.9.2[b]	System access and credentials are terminated consistent with personnel actions such as termination or transfer.					
3.9.2[c]	The system is protected during and after personnel transfer actions.					

Control #	Description	Assessment of Method*	Document (e.g. SSP or Co. Procedure Guide)	Page #	Reviewed by	Validated By
Physical Security (PP)						
3.10.1	**Limit physical access to organizational information systems, equipment, and the respective operating environments to authorized individuals**					
3.10.1[a]	Authorized individuals allowed physical access are identified.					
3.10.1[b]	Physical access to organizational systems is limited to authorized individuals.					
3.10.1[c]	Physical access to equipment is limited to authorized individuals.					
3.10.1[d]	Physical access to operating environments is limited to authorized individuals.					
3.10.2	**Protect and monitor the physical facility and support infrastructure for those information systems**					
3.10.2[a]	The physical facility where organizational systems reside is protected.					
3.10.2[b]	The support infrastructure for					

	organizational systems is protected.	
3.10.2[c]	The physical facility where organizational systems reside is monitored.	
3.10.2[d]	The support infrastructure for organizational systems is monitored.	
3.10.3	**Escort visitors and monitor visitor activity**	
3.10.3[a]	Visitors are escorted.	
3.10.3[b]	Visitor activity is monitored.	
3.10.4	**Maintain audit logs of physical access**	
3.10.5	**Control and manage physical access devices**	
3.10.5[a]	Physical access devices are identified.	
3.10.5[b]	Physical access devices are controlled.	
3.10.5[c]	Physical access devices are managed.	
3.10.6	**Enforce safeguarding measures for CUI at alternate work sites (e.g., telework sites)**	
3.10.6[a]	Safeguarding measures for CUI are defined for alternate work sites.	
3.10.6[b]	Safeguarding measures for CUI are enforced for alternate work sites.	

Control #	Description	Assessment Method*	Document (e.g., SSP or Co Procedure Control)	Page #	Review ed By	Validat ed By
Risk Assessments (RA)						
3.11.1	**Periodically assess the risk to organizational operations (including mission, functions, image, or reputation), organizational assets, and individuals, resulting from the operation of organizational information systems and the associated processing, storage, or transmission of CUI**					
3.11.1[a]	The frequency to assess risk to organizational operations, organizational assets, and individuals is defined.					
3.11.1[b]	Risk to organizational operations, organizational assets, and individuals resulting from the operation of an organizational system that processes, stores, or transmits CUI is assessed with the defined frequency.					

3.11.2	**Scan for vulnerabilities in the information system and applications periodically and when new vulnerabilities affecting the system are identified**	
3.11.2[a]	The frequency to scan for vulnerabilities in organizational systems and applications is defined.	
3.11.2[b]	Vulnerability scans are performed on organizational systems with the defined frequency.	
3.11.2[c]	Vulnerability scans are performed on applications with the defined frequency.	
3.11.2[d]	Vulnerability scans are performed on organizational systems when new vulnerabilities are identified.	
3.11.2[e]	Vulnerability scans are performed on applications when new vulnerabilities are identified.	
3.11.3	**Remediate vulnerabilities in accordance with assessments of risk**	
3.11.3[a]	Vulnerabilities are identified.	
3.11.3[b]	Vulnerabilities are remediated in	

	accordance with risk assessments.	

Control #	Description	Assessment Method*	Document (e.g., SSP or Co. Procedure Guide)	Page #	Reviewed By	Validated By
Security Assessments (SA)						
3.12.1	**Periodically assess the security controls in organizational information systems to determine if the controls are effective in their application**					
3.12.1[a]	The frequency of security control assessments is defined.					
3.12.1[b]	Security controls are assessed with the defined frequency to determine if the controls are effective in their application.					
3.12.2	**Develop and implement plans of action designed to correct deficiencies and reduce or eliminate vulnerabilities in organizational information systems**					
3.12.2[a]	Deficiencies and vulnerabilities to be addressed by the plan of action are identified.					
3.12.2[b]	A plan of action is developed to correct identified deficiencies and reduce or eliminate identified vulnerabilities.					
3.12.2[c]	The plan of action is implemented to correct identified deficiencies and reduce or eliminate identified vulnerabilities.					
3.12.3	**Monitor information system security controls on an ongoing basis to**					

	ensure the continued effectiveness of the controls	
3.12.4	Develop, document, and periodically update system security plans that describe system boundaries, system environments of operation, how security requirements are implemented, and the relationships with or connections to other systems	
3.12.4[a]	A system security plan is developed.	
3.12.4[b]	The system boundary is described and documented in the system security plan.	
3.12.4[c]	The system environment of operation is described and documented in the system security plan.	
3.12.4[d]	The security requirements identified and approved by the designated authority as non-applicable are identified.	
3.12.4[e]	The method of security requirement implementation is described and documented in the system security plan.	
3.12.4[f]	The relationship with or connection to other systems is described and documented in the system security plan.	
3.12.4[g]	The frequency to update the system security plan is defined.	
3.12.4[h]	System security plan is updated with the defined frequency.	

Control #	Description	Assessment Method*	Document (i.e. SSP or Co. Procedure Guide)	Page #	Reviewed By	Validated By
System & Communications Protection (SC)						
3.13.1	**Monitor, control, and protect organizational communications (i.e., information transmitted or received by organizational information systems) at the external boundaries and key internal boundaries of the information systems**					
3.13.1[a]	The external system boundary is defined.					
3.13.1[b]	Key internal system boundaries are defined.					
3.13.1[c]	Communications are monitored at the external system boundary.					
3.13.1[d]	Communications are monitored at key internal boundaries.					
3.13.1[e]	Communications are controlled at the external system boundary.					
3.13.1[f]	Communications are controlled at key internal boundaries.					
3.13.1[g]	Communications are protected at the external system boundary.					
3.13.1[h]	Communications are protected at key internal boundaries.					
3.13.2	**Employ architectural designs, software development**					

	techniques, and systems engineering principles that promote effective information security within organizational information systems	
3.13.2[a]	Architectural designs that promote effective information security are identified.	
3.13.2[b]	Software development techniques that promote effective information security are identified.	
3.13.2[c]	Systems engineering principles that promote effective information security are identified.	
3.13.2[d]	Identified architectural designs that promote effective information security are employed.	
3.13.2[e]	Identified software development techniques that promote effective information security are employed.	
3.13.2[f]	Identified systems engineering principles that promote effective information security are employed.	
3.13.3	Separate user functionality from information system management functionality	
3.13.3[a]	User functionality is identified.	
3.13.3[b]	System management functionality is identified.	
3.13.3[c]	User functionality is separated from system management functionality.	
3.13.4	Prevent unauthorized and unintended information transfer	

	via shared system resources	
3.13.5	**Implement subnetworks for publicly accessible system components that are physically or logically separated from internal networks**	
3.13.5[a]	Publicly accessible system components are identified.	
3.13.5[b]	Subnetworks for publicly accessible system components are physically or logically separated from internal networks.	
3.13.6	**Deny network communications traffic by default and allow network communications traffic by exception (i.e., deny all, permit by exception)**	
3.13.6[a]	Network communications traffic is denied by default.	
3.13.6[b]	Network communications traffic is allowed by exception.	
3.13.7	**Prevent remote devices from simultaneously establishing non-remote connections with the information system and communicating via some other connection to resources in external networks**	

Control #	Description	Assessment Method*	Document (e.g., SSP or Co. Procedure Guide)	Page #	Reviewed By	Validated By
System & Communications Protection (SC)						
3.13.8	**Implement cryptographic mechanisms to prevent unauthorized disclosure of CUI during transmission unless otherwise protected by alternative physical safeguards**					
3.13.8[a]	Cryptographic mechanisms intended to prevent unauthorized disclosure of CUI are identified.					
3.13.8[b]	Alternative physical safeguards intended to prevent unauthorized disclosure of CUI are identified.					
3.13.8[c]	Either cryptographic mechanisms or alternative physical safeguards are implemented to prevent unauthorized disclosure of CUI during transmission.					
3.13.9	**Terminate network connections associated with communications sessions at the end of the sessions or after a defined period of inactivity**					
3.13.9[a]	A period of inactivity to terminate network connections associated with communications sessions is defined.					

3.13.9[b]	Network connections associated with communications sessions are terminated at the end of the sessions.	
3.13.9[c]	Network connections associated with communications sessions are terminated after the defined period of inactivity.	
3.13.10	**Establish and manage cryptographic keys for cryptography employed in the information system**	
3.13.10[a]	Cryptographic keys are established whenever cryptography is employed.	
3.13.10[b]	Cryptographic keys are managed whenever cryptography is employed.	
3.13.11	**Employ FIPS-validated cryptography when used to protect the confidentiality of CUI**	
3.13.12	**Prohibit remote activation of collaborative computing devices and provide indication of devices in use to users present at the device**	
3.13.12[a]	Collaborative computing devices are identified.	
3.13.12[b]	Collaborative computing devices provide indication to users of devices in use.	

3.13.12[c]	Remote activation of collaborative computing devices is prohibited.	
3.13.13	**Control and monitor the use of mobile code**	
3.13.13[a]	Use of mobile code is controlled.	
3.13.13[b]	Use of mobile code is monitored.	
3.13.14	**Control and monitor the use of Voice over Internet Protocol (VoIP) technologies**	
3.13.14[a]	Use of Voice over Internet Protocol (VoIP) technologies is controlled.	
3.13.14[b]	Use of Voice over Internet Protocol (VoIP) technologies is monitored.	
3.13.15	**Protect the authenticity of communications sessions**	
3.13.16	**Protect the confidentiality of CUI at rest**	

Control #	Description	Assessment Method*	Document	Page #	Reviewed By	Validated By
System & Information Integrity (SI)						
3.14.1	**Identify, report, and correct information and information system flaws in a timely manner**					
3.14.1[a]	The time within which to identify system flaws is specified.					
3.14.1[b]	System flaws are identified within the specified time frame.					
3.14.1[c]	The time within which to report system flaws is specified.					
3.14.1[d]	System flaws are reported within the specified time frame.					
3.14.1[e]	The time within which to correct system flaws is specified.					
3.14.1[f]	System flaws are corrected within the specified time frame.					
3.14.2	**Provide protection from malicious code at appropriate locations within organizational information systems**					
3.14.2[a]	Designated locations for malicious code protection are identified.					
3.14.2[b]	Protection from malicious code at designated locations is provided.					
3.14.3	**Monitor information system security alerts and**					

	advisories and take appropriate actions in response
3.14.3[a]	Response actions to system security alerts and advisories are identified.
3.14.3[b]	System security alerts and advisories are monitored.
3.14.3[c]	Actions in response to system security alerts and advisories are taken.
3.14.4	Update malicious code protection mechanisms when new releases are available
3.14.5	Perform periodic scans of the information system and real-time scans of files from external sources as files are downloaded, opened, or executed
3.14.5[a]	The frequency for malicious code scans is defined.
3.14.5[b]	Malicious code scans are performed with the defined frequency.
3.14.5[c]	Real-time malicious code scans of files from external sources as files are downloaded, opened, or executed are performed.
3.14.6	Monitor the information system including inbound and

	outbound communications traffic, to detect attacks and indicators of potential attacks	
3.14.6[a]	The system is monitored to detect attacks and indicators of potential attacks.	
3.14.6[b]	Inbound communications traffic is monitored to detect attacks and indicators of potential attacks.	
3.14.6[c]	Outbound communications traffic is monitored to detect attacks and indicators of potential attacks.	
3.14.7	Identify unauthorized use of the information system	
3.14.7[a]	Authorized use of the system is defined.	
3.14.7[b]	Unauthorized use of the system is identified.	

About the Author

Dr. Russo is an internationally published author, and his work has been published in four foreign languages and English. He is a former Senior Information Security Engineer within the Department of Defense's (DOD) F-35 Joint Strike Fighter program. He has an extensive background in cybersecurity and is an expert in the Risk Management Framework (RMF) and DOD Instruction 8510, which implement RMF throughout the DOD and the federal government. He holds a Certified Information Systems Security Professional (CISSP) certification and a CISSP in information security architecture (ISSAP). He has a 2017 certification as a Chief Information Security Officer (CISO) from the National Defense University, Washington, DC. He retired from the US Army Reserves in 2012 as the Senior Intelligence Officer.

Dr. Russo's credentials in cybersecurity...

He is the former CISO at the Department of Education wherein 2016, he led the effort to close over 95% of the outstanding US Congressional and Inspector General cybersecurity shortfall weaknesses spanning as far back as five years.

Dr. Russo is the former Senior Cybersecurity Engineer supporting the Joint Medical Logistics Development Functional Center of the Defense Health Agency (DHA) at Fort Detrick, MD. He led a team of engineering and cybersecurity professionals protecting five major Medical Logistics systems supporting over 200 DOD Medical Treatment Facilities around the globe.

In 2011, Dr. Russo was certified by the Office of Personnel Management as a graduate of the Senior Executive Service (SES) Candidate program.

From 2009 through 2011, Dr. Russo was the Chief Technology Officer at the Small Business Administration (SBA). He led a team of over 100 IT professionals in supporting an intercontinental Enterprise IT infrastructure and security operations spanning 12-time zones; he deployed cutting-edge technologies to enhance SBA's business and information sharing operations supporting the small business community. Dr. Russo was the first-ever Program Executive Officer (PEO)/Senior Program Manager in the Office of Intelligence & Analysis at Headquarters, Department of Homeland Security (DHS), Washington, DC. He was responsible for developing and deploying secure Information and Intelligence support *systems for OI&A to include software applications and systems to enhance the DHS mission. He was responsible for the program management development lifecycle during his tenure at DHS.*

He holds a Master of Science from the National Defense University in Government Information Leadership with a concentration in Cybersecurity and a Bachelor of Arts in Political Science with a minor in Russian Studies from Lehigh University. He holds Level III Defense Acquisition certification in Program Management, Information Technology, and Systems Engineering. He has been a member of the DOD Acquisition Corps since 2001.

Other Books by the Author

System Security Plan (SSP) Template & Workbook NIST-based

https://www.amazon.com/System-Security-Plan-Template-Workbook-ebook/dp/B07BCY41D2/ref=sr_1_1?ie=UTF8&qid=1523490730&sr=8-1&keywords=system+security+plan

NIST 800-171: Writing an Effective Plan of Action & Milestones (POAM)

https://www.amazon.com/NIST-800-171-Milestones-Understanding-Responsibilities-ebook/dp/B07C9T3ZCT/ref=sr_1_1?ie=UTF8&qid=1523491061&sr=8-1&keywords=plan+of+action+and+milestone

www.ingramcontent.com/pod-product-compliance
Lightning Source LLC
LaVergne TN
LVHW051241050326
832903LV00028B/2504